LIFE LESSONS FOR THE
Teenage
GIRL

LIFE LESSONS FOR THE
Teenage
GIRL

*Quotes, Inspiration and Advice
for Women by Women*

Kelly Tonelli

New York

LIFE LESSONS FOR THE Teenage **GIRL**
Quotes, Inspiration and Advice for Women by Women

Published in New York, New York, by Morgan James Publishing. Morgan James and The Entrepreneurial Publisher are trademarks of Morgan James, LLC.
www.MorganJamesPublishing.com

The Morgan James Speakers Group can bring authors to your live event. For more information or to book an event visit The Morgan James Speakers Group at
www.TheMorganJamesSpeakersGroup.com.

A **free** eBook edition is available with the purchase of this print book.

ISBN 978-1-63047-202-3 paperback
ISBN 978-1-63047-203-0 eBook
ISBN 978-1-63047-204-7 hardcover
Library of Congress Control Number:
2014935074

CLEARLY PRINT YOUR NAME ABOVE IN UPPER CASE

Instructions to claim your free eBook edition:
1. Download the BitLit app for Android or iOS
2. Write your name in **UPPER CASE** on the line
3. Use the BitLit app to submit a photo
4. Download your eBook to any device

Cover Design by:
Chris Treccani
www.3dogdesign.net

Interior Design by:
Bonnie Bushman
bonnie@caboodlegraphics.com

In an effort to support local communities, raise awareness and funds, Morgan James Publishing donates a percentage of all book sales for the life of each book to Habitat for Humanity Peninsula and Greater Williamsburg.

Get involved today, visit
www.MorganJamesBuilds.com.

Habitat for Humanity®
Peninsula and
Greater Williamsburg
Building Partner

For my husband, Jason,
and our daughter, Charlie

TABLE OF CONTENTS

Acknowledgments   ix

Introduction   xi

Chapter 1   Self-Esteem   1
Maybe you really are good enough

Chapter 2   Relationships   18
Being with others and still liking yourself

Chapter 3   Goals   39
Deciding what the heck to do
next and making it happen

Chapter 4   Instincts   55
Listening to that little voice
that tells you what to do

Chapter 5   Career   72
Please don't tell me I have to
live with my parents forever!

Chapter 6   Finances   85
What to do with all of your fabulous loot
and how to avoid going broke

Chapter 7   Failure and Rejection   99
Ouch, that hurts! Now what?

Chapter 8   Finding Your Moral Compass   112
*You have to believe in something
(but you get to pick)*

Chapter 9   The Future   126
What the heck do I do now?

Conclusion   147
About the Author   152
Index   153

ACKNOWLEDGMENTS

I want to thank all of the successful, talented, and incredibly generous women who carved time out of their terribly busy schedules to contribute to this book. It is my hope that their words will offer comfort, guidance, and inspiration to anyone who reads them, and that my own commentary does not in any way take away from the power of their words.

I especially want to thank Kat Graham, Temple Grandin, and Vanna White. These women were the first to offer their contributions to this book and gave me hope that this book might be possible after all, even though I had no budget and even less street cred.

Life Lessons for the Teenage Girl could not have been completed without the love and support of my best friend and husband, Jason. Time and time again you show me that you love me (and, more importantly, like me) no matter what.

Our daughter, Charlie, is my inspiration. She amazes me on a daily basis with her heart, her intelligence, and her love for life. I can only hope that she will still be willing to be seen with me in public when she is a teenager. Fingers crossed.

Jason and my mom, Patricia Pank, also spent innumerable hours reading and rereading this book to catch my many errors. There were a lot. Any that remain are solely my fault.

I want to thank my mom for teaching me the value of hard work and the importance of knowing I can be independent, even when I don't have to be.

Finally, I would like to thank the teenage girls with whom I have had the privilege of working with in my practice. You have blessed me with your stories and have motivated me to try and find alternative ways to be helpful to you and to deserve your trust.

INTRODUCTION

In my professional life, I'm a psychologist and frequently get the privilege of working with teenage girls like you. I'm constantly amazed by the strength you show in overcoming life's difficulties. Sometimes, though, you get just a bit lost. I know you're not stupid. You're far from stupid as a matter of fact. You're so much savvier than I was at your age (eons and eons ago, but, despite what my daughter thinks, there were no dinosaurs). Despite your obviously superior smarts, many of the challenges I faced during my teen years continue to frustrate you and your friends today. A primary struggle may be knowing which people you can believe in and trust. Who can you look to for advice when you're struggling? Often you may not want to discuss your problems with your parents—it's

OK; that's how it's supposed to be. You're learning how to find your own way and can't do that if you're looking to your mom and dad for everything.

I frequently hear that parents can't relate any longer and are too old to understand. Unfortunately, your parents do sometimes know what they're talking about, and you may miss out on that guidance. It may be incredibly hard to believe, but your parents were actually teenagers once dealing with love and friendships, parents, and problems much the same as you are now. Your mom may be able to understand what it's like to get your heart broken and tell you how she got through it when it happened to her. You dad might have had a jerk teacher who treated him like crap and may be able to talk with you about how he handled it.

So, if not your parents, where else can you turn? Can you look to your friends? Well, they can be a source of phenomenal support and may be insightful in many ways—they're in the trenches with you and can relate in ways others may not be able to. The trouble is that they don't necessarily have any more life experience than you do. There's something that can be gained from learning from those who have gone before you. So… where do you go?

Frequently, this insight may come from celebrities. These can be people older than you who have had more life experiences than you—all good, right? Well, maybe. The problem is that articles about them rarely contain any real advice. In interviews they are asked about fashion, how they stay thin, and the details of their love lives. These topics may make you feel worse rather than better. All too often the details of the celebrities' lives are glamorized, which may cause you to feel as though your own life is insignificant. Articles discuss the exciting places where they travel or the other celebrities they date. Some will discuss the fitness regimens the celebrities use to stay in shape, but it will fail to acknowledge their personal trainers or chefs who prepare their meals.

How are you supposed to feel like you can compete? Celebrities are also rarely asked real questions in their interviews that real people can relate to. Maybe they'll be asked what guidance they might give someone who is trying to break into their industry. Helpful to some, but most of you are not planning a career in the entertainment industry. It also fails to account for women who have achieved success in other industries (for example, business, politics, and sports).

That is where I got the idea for this book. I wanted to ask these successful women what advice shaped them during their teen years or for a piece of advice they wish they'd received when they were teenagers. I left the topic wide open for these women—they were free to write about whatever they wanted. I wanted this book to include women from a variety of industries as well as backgrounds. I wanted to include women whose names might be immediately recognizable to you because they're actresses (like Kat Graham) or musicians (like Elie Golding), but I also wanted to include women you may have never heard of but definitely should, including politicians (like Janet Nguyen or Mimi Walters) and businesswomen (like Becky Quick).

You may be wondering how I picked these specific women in the first place and how they went from my dream list to actual participants in the book. This was trickier than you might think—it definitely was harder than I thought it would be. Initially, I brainstormed a list of women who I thought would have something useful to contribute. I searched the Internet and picked the brains of my friends and family. I made a list of their agents, business managers, public relations team, attorneys, personal assistants, and corporate contacts.

I then did something somewhat boneheaded. I mailed these contact people a letter explaining the project and why their person should participate. Interestingly, I learned almost no one reads letters anymore—especially unsolicited letters from a complete stranger (me). When I received little feedback from the letters, I realized email would be simpler. I again scoured the Internet to get contact information for those same agents, managers, and publicists, etc., and emailed a similar letter explaining the project. A few more responses began trickling in. Then I remembered the joy that is Twitter. I began tweeting like an idiot, trying to explain the project in 140 characters or less to women who have thousands of followers. This was key. Responses began flooding in.

So why would these amazingly successful women take time out of their busy schedules to participate in this project? Well, it definitely wasn't for the money. There was none. They didn't get a dime for their time and efforts. They did it for two reasons: First, they care about you. These women wanted to offer guidance to you as you navigate the difficult teen years. They also wanted you to know that you are not alone in your struggles; they've been there too and made it through to the other side. You can survive it too. The second reason was these wonderful women care about charity. I'm donating

50 percent of any royalties received to Children's Hospital Los Angeles (CHLA).

CHLA is a nonprofit hospital that depends on generous donations to help heal children in an environment that lets them thrive. Each year, more than 96,000 sick children come to the hospital for care. I worked at CHLA for a number of years and was consistently awestruck at the quality of care they were able to provide, and I wanted to find a way to contribute to that care. These women saw contributing to this book as a way to also contribute to CHLA. Follow the examples of these amazing women and find ways to give back. You can volunteer your time (or money) to a good cause (anyone you like) and Pay It Forward. You too can positively impact the lives of others.

All of the direct quotes that appear in this book appear entirely as I received them. They weren't edited for content.

Chapter 1

SELF-ESTEEM

*Maybe you really
are good enough*

~~~~~~~~~~~~~~~~~~~~

Okay, let's talk about self-esteem. What is it? Simply put, your self-esteem is how you feel about yourself and your overall value to the world. People who are said to have high self-esteem feel positively about themselves, while people who have low self-esteem feel bad about themselves. Unfortunately, people often confuse high self-esteem with arrogance or being full of yourself. Not the case at all, my dears. There's a big difference between confidence, or high self-esteem, and arrogance. Someone who is arrogant uses their confidence to make others feel bad. There's an "evil" intent. You can feel good about yourself without being a jerk. You can feel good about you without being mean to others or bragging about your many accomplishments to make others feel bad about themselves. Often, the most confident person in the room is the quietest about their achievements.

A concrete example may help explain self-esteem better. Most of you have seen the movie (or read the book) *Twilight*, right? Brief recap—Bella moves to Washington to live with her dad and meets Edward, a vampire. They fall in love and encounter a series of barriers to this love. Now, you may be asking yourself what this has to do with self-esteem. Give me a sec. See, *Twilight* has three female characters who demonstrate different types or levels of self-esteem. We'll start with Bella, our heroine. She's typically viewed as having low self-esteem. She frequently refers to herself as clumsy and plain. She constantly states she's not good enough or attractive enough for Edward. She struggles to understand why he's with her. You can see how this might lead someone to allow others to treat them poorly.

Now Edward's "sister," Alice, on the other hand, demonstrates healthy self-esteem. She accepts herself with all her quirks and is able to accept the same in others. She's comfortable enough in her own skin not to feel threatened by or have disdain for others. Inflated self-esteem is demonstrated by Edward's other "sister," Rosalie, who's described as self-centered and vain. She shows contempt for those who are different from her and feels she's better than everyone else. Fortunately, she grows and matures during the series.

Where does self-esteem come from? It comes from you, but it is influenced by a number of people/places in your life. Self-esteem is formed by the messages you receive from the authority figures in your life (like your parents) and how they teach you to celebrate your strengths and support your weaknesses (we all have them). It's influenced by whether you're able to find activities in which you can feel successful—whether in school or through outside interests.

Your self-esteem may be affected by the reactions from your peers and whether or not you feel accepted by them. Most importantly, your self-esteem is impacted by the way you interpret this data and how it's internalized. The healthier your self-esteem, the better able you are to handle your own mistakes and tolerate the potential disapproval of others. The more fragile your self-esteem, the more likely you are to take on others' negative opinions as fact and see your mistakes as failures.

Self-esteem does not always make sense. There are many girls out there who seem to have it all: they're good students, have amazing friends, and thrive in their activities, but they still may feel bad about themselves. No matter what they achieve, they don't feel they are good enough. They're always trying to achieve more, and do more, to prove their worth. Other people around them may have no idea that they have low self-esteem. It's not always obvious to everyone else. Many put on a brave face despite being very hard on themselves, and they protect that fragile self-esteem like a closely guarded secret. They do this so others will not know they're struggling. Often they fear being perceived as broken or damaged. Like out in the wild, in high school the weak are killed and eaten.

Everyone has insecure feelings regardless of outside appearances. Believe in yourself, create your own happiness.

Tory Burch—American fashion designer, businesswoman, philanthropist

It's so important to remember that everyone feels bad about themselves sometimes. You can never truly guess how someone else feels about herself. It's easy to assume the girl that you think "has it all" must feel like a superstar, but she may have just as many (or more) doubts about herself as you do. Oftentimes we hold ourselves up to some standard that's unattainable or impossible to achieve. In my practice, I often hear clients say that they wish they could be as confident as Rachel or as popular as Maria (names changed to protect privacy). What I often remind them is that they have no idea what's going on in that person's life. You don't know who has an eating disorder, or a father with cancer, or an abusive mother. It's important to focus on yourself and what you can do to make yourself happy. Comparing yourself to others rarely leads to a positive outcome.

There's a great danger in building your self-esteem on the opinions of others. People are fickle. They might think you're amazing today, which might make you feel great about yourself. But what happens when their preference changes? If they're not as into you, your self-esteem can flatten like a pancake. Look at many of the former child stars, for example. When they were on a hit show and had thousands of screaming fans chanting their names, they were on top of the world. But what happens when those fans move on to the next big thing or their hit show reaches its inevitable conclusion?

I hate to throw her under the bus, but look at Lindsay Lohan. She was an extremely successful child and teen star, but when it started to fall apart she panicked. This is a "What came first: the chicken or the egg?" type of situation. Did the panic about her waning fame cause her to turn to drugs and alcohol, or did her substance abuse lead to her declining career. No one knows the answer to this, but as her career plummeted, she engaged in increasingly erratic behaviors aimed at recapturing the public's attention and adoration. (Look at Justin Bieber's recent actions to see someone who is teetering on the edge of these behaviors).

This situation is tough no matter what, but those who based their self-esteem primarily on their perception of their own strengths will survive better than those whose self-esteem is built on the opinions of others. I often think this is why some celebrities are able to transition better than others. Those whose self-esteem takes a nosedive seem to make increasingly desperate steps to regain the public's attention. Miley Cyrus' Video Music Award (VMA) performance in 2013 comes to mind. I don't know her personally, but it seemed to me she was so desperate to show the world she was no longer Hannah Montana, and to recreate herself in a more "mature" way, that she nearly prostituted herself on national TV.

This seems to happen fairly often, think of Christina Aguilera during her "Dirty" phase or Britney Spears during her Kevin Federline days. Each young woman was trying to separate herself from her previous pop star image while maintaining the media's attention. In your life, you don't want to be that girl. Choose your actions based on your own value structure, not to get the attention and acceptance of others. Find your own happiness and try not to rely on others to confirm your value.

If I could offer the teenage me some advice I guess I would've said that everything was going to get easier. That love and heartbreak, school, really everything will one day be just a memory and to not get too upset when you feel that people let you down. That your friends, your parents and everyone are human and they're going to all mess up and to not think they are. That what you read in magazines and see on TV isn't real. That it's sometimes the furthest thing from reality. That the kind of life you'll have will be much more dynamic if you don't try and put things and people into a box. I'd tell myself to take the pressure off. That the only person I need to make happy in the end is me. I would've told myself the same thing I tell myself now, that it's ok to be different and who cares what they think, no really, who gives a damn. It's you in the end that has to live with yourself, not your mom, your boyfriend ... your best friend or the star on TV. It's you in the end. Love yourself, stay real with yourself, and fight your battles alone. No one will fight them for you.

Kat Graham—actress, model, singer and dancer

There is so much good stuff in here! First, I would like to emphasize the part about what you read in magazines and see on TV isn't real. Let me repeat that part—it is NOT real. These are situations where people spend hours being worked on by amazingly talented hair and makeup professionals who know how to play up their best parts while hiding the ugly bits. They're then put in front of a camera with the kindest forms of lighting, again designed to emphasize their best characteristics. After the pictures are taken (or the film is shot), the images are edited further to remove any possible blemish. How can the average girl compete with this kind of "perfection"? Well, she can't and shouldn't even try. The only person you can truly compete with is yourself.

You can start by trying to become the best possible you that you can be. If you want to get better grades, make a plan about how that can happen. Do you need to spend more time studying? Do you need to find someone to tutor you and help you out? If you want to become a faster swimmer, make a plan. Do you need to take more lessons from a coach? Do you need to cross-train with another sport? In all of these situations, you're only competing against yourself—trying to find ways to improve yourself. It isn't fair to compare yourself against another girl at school or on TV. Comparing yourself against others often leads to low self-esteem and feeling bad about you as a whole.

In my work with teenage girls, I have encountered quite a few with eating disorders. The most common two are Anorexia Nervosa and Bulimia Nervosa. These are complicated disorders with a number of defining criteria, but I'm going to simplify it here for time's sake. Anorexia is typically a disorder where someone refuses to eat (or eats very little) in order to lose weight or avoid gaining weight. Bulimia is when someone eats large amounts of food and then engages in some behavior to get rid of the eaten food (throwing up, laxatives, and excessive exercise, for example). Often these young women, who are being challenged by their eating disorders, compare themselves negatively to others. They think others are smarter, prettier, funnier, and thinner. Focus on being the happiest you can be and do your best not to compare that girl to others. You can't control anyone but you, and part of being the best you that you can be is to be healthy.

Something else that Kat said really resonated with me. She talked about how you are the only one that you really need to please because you are the one who ultimately has to live with you. Now, I'm not telling you to tell everyone in your life to go take a flying leap or anything, but in the end it really is about whether you can live with the choices you have made. This comes down to who you choose as friends, activities you participate in, and how you do in school. Are you comfortable with the choices you've made, and can you tolerate the consequences of those choices? If you can, then forget what anyone else has to say about it. They should keep their big mouths shut. If you're uncomfortable with your choices or can't tolerate the consequences, then it's time to change the way you're living your life. Find choices and consequences you can live with.

When I was in high school, I was a total mess. Every decision I made seemed based on whether or not everyone else (usually kids at school) would approve. I even hung out with the friends that I thought I was supposed to (even though I didn't particularly like them all). I did OK in school, but not too well, so people wouldn't think I was a geek, and I spent hours agonizing over what I was going to wear to school each morning. If any of you could see pictures of me from high school, you'd be shocked that I spent a lot of time worrying about my clothes—I looked "odd" much of the time, but that was the style of the early '90s. It wasn't pretty, and I hope no one ever feels the need to bring it back.

I agree with Kat. If I could do it over, I'd try to care less about what other people thought was right for me and focus on what felt right to me. I might focus on the people I really liked and the activities I thought were interesting. Remember, once you leave high school you'll have the choice to continue your friendships or let them lapse. Many people you'll never see again, unless you opt to attend the same high school reunion. Their approval or disapproval won't have any long term impact on your life. You'll have the opportunity to move on and meet new people, if you so choose.

> I would tell teens to be #BANJI that means Be Authentic Never Jeopardize Individuality! BE YOU! Don't follow! Just lead.
>
> **Missy Elliot**—rapper, singer-songwriter, record producer, dancer, actress

This ties in very nicely with the quote from Kat Graham. Missy stresses the importance of being you and being confident in who that person is. This means participating in the activities that you like, listening to the music you enjoy, wearing the clothes that fit your personal style, choosing friends you enjoy hanging out with, and so much more. All too often in high school there develops a kind of "group think" where there is a general consensus about what is acceptable. "We" like these brands and shop in these stores and all listen to the same music. What Missy is telling you is that it's OK to say "no thanks" to the status quo. It's OK to discover a new band and develop your own personal style—even if everyone else might not "get" it.

Is everyone going to love it? Nope. Some people will have a hard time with you choosing to be different. They may give you a hard time. People who are really insecure may give you a very hard time. People with low self-esteem tend to struggle with people who aren't like them. They bully others to feel better. They tear others down to make themselves feel taller and stronger. Pretty sad, right? Here's the important thing to remember: People with good self-esteem can tolerate differences. They are confident enough in their own choices not to be threatened when your life is different from theirs. Remember this.

If someone is giving you a hard time, they're scared. They might not even know it, but you will. You can find strength from this knowledge. Use that knowledge to carry you through. This will be the case throughout your life. If someone is threatened by your (or someone else's) differences, then they're not confident in their own beliefs. Use this to strengthen your own position. Don't allow others to cause you to question your own beliefs through the volume they're willing to yell about their beliefs. You're as entitled to your thoughts, feelings, and beliefs as anyone else.

Don't look externally to find self-worth. It must come from within. Translation: don't rely on boys to tell you how great you are.

Jenny McCarthy—model, actress, author, activist, and game show host

Huge! Do you notice a similar theme running through the various quotes from these amazing women? Jenny stresses the importance of finding your self-worth within yourself rather than relying on others to give it to you. Let me give you an example—I was seeing a beautiful high school student who had been happily dating a classmate for about a year. She reported that the year of dating had been wonderful, and she couldn't imagine being happier than she had been during that year. Her boyfriend told her that she was gorgeous and smart and funny, and, while they were together, she believed him. You can imagine what happened, right? Well, they broke up and suddenly she felt worthless. Her entire self-esteem had been built on the opinion of this young man and once he no longer valued her, she didn't value herself.

I have seen this happen in a variety of ways. Teenagers who are excellent students will often base their self-esteem on getting good grades. This is fine until the day they encounter a class (or professor) that's challenging. They can begin to have doubts about their abilities, and the foundation on which their self-esteem is based begins to crumble. No matter how smart you are, you may not get all A's. No matter how funny you are, someone someday won't laugh. You can't base your worth on them.

What are you supposed to do about it? One thing you can do is base your self-esteem on internal factors, for instance, "I'm smart" instead of "I get good grades" or "I'm a good person" versus "Scott likes me." You need to base your opinion of your self-worth on you, not on what others think of you. Sometimes you may need to remind yourself that you don't have to be perfect to earn your good self-esteem. You don't have to always earn the highest grades to know that you're smart. There are circumstances outside of your control. Your brilliance won't always equal A's.

You don't have to always be liked by everyone to know that you're a good person and are fun to be around. I'm going to recommend that you take care with absolutes—nearly everyone will fail at them. Perfection doesn't exist. When you demand it from yourself, you're setting yourself up for disappointment. An example of an absolute would be, "I must get all A's to prove that I'm smart." I've known in my many years people who were absolutely brilliant who didn't receive all A's just as I have known some that weren't that bright who did.

> The sun does not rise and set with what others think of you.
>
> **Erika Bearman**—PR girl for Oscar de la Renta

Erika Bearman echoes the sentiment shared by Jenny McCarthy —you can't give too much power to what other people think about you. Their opinions of you aren't necessarily reliable and are subject to interpretation and their own biases.

Let me give you an example from my practice (I've changed important information to protect the privacy of the innocent and the guilty). I was seeing a high school junior who was coming in to talk about her difficulties with anxiety. During one of our discussions, she began to go on a tear about another girl at the school. She began to rip this girl up one side and down the other—she was stupid, "not that pretty," and a slut. With further discussion, my client shared that the other girl was also "hanging out" with a guy my client liked. It became apparent that this was the true reason why my client didn't like her. If this girl had accepted my client's opinion as fact, she would've taken on the labels of stupid, not pretty, and slut.

Please, please, please remember this. Just because someone (even a bunch of "someones") decides to label you, you don't need to accept that label. Take in what others say to determine if it has any validity. If it's crap, discard it and move on. If it's true, decide if you're satisfied with that label. If you are, move on. If its' true and you don't like it, think about ways to make changes.

> I think being confident in who you are, and truly learning to love yourself and focus on the possibilities that lie ahead.
>
> **Kaitlyn Jenkins**—actress, dancer

You're the only person who can determine your worth. Others may try to puff you up or tear you down, but it will be your decision whether to accept or reject their contributions to your life. Let's talk about unconditional love. The most important form of unconditional love is the love you can have for yourself. You can love yourself even when you make mistakes—"warts and all." This will give you the confidence to go out in the world and try new things (even when they might not work—Failure, chapter 7). Focus on the future and know you'll always have at least one person in your corner—you.

Your dreams for the future can carry you through the hard times. Knowing what you're working toward (and dreaming of) can make even the crappiest of current circumstances bearable. If you're having a rough day, week, month, or year, consider what lies ahead and think about how much better it will be. Optimism doesn't have to be delusional—sometimes it's just finding a way to keep it positive. Focus on how great it will be when you live in New York City, or are off to college, or travel the world—whatever/wherever you hope to be one day.

Stay true to yourself, no matter what the trends would dictate.

Samantha Ronson—singer-songwriter, DJ

You're going to be tempted to try on different identities while you're figuring out who you are now or will become in the future. This is completely natural. The important caveat is that you want to be able to recognize yourself each time you look in the mirror. In the world we live in, there will always be trends and there will always be those who follow them blindly. Trends are not always a bad thing—I followed a few in my time (many I'm now not so proud to admit). The crucial piece is that you need to still be yourself.

When I was in eighth or ninth grade, I went through this sort of Goth phase (kind of like the emo kids of today) where I wore a lot of black clothing, had pale skin, and wore dark makeup. Many would be surprised to hear this now as I'm now neither Goth nor emo. The reason this fit for me is because I was going through an emotional time that I didn't really know how to handle. I was expressing my inner turmoil through my fashion (such that it was). It fit me at that time.

This is the part that's important. Stay true to who you are. At the time, it would've been ridiculous for me to dress any other way as it wouldn't have been appropriate to where I was. Make sure what you're doing fits who and where you are—not just what the magazines (or your friends) say you should be doing. It's an important part of getting comfortable in your own skin.

Feeling good about being you:

1. Take a page out of the book of Stuart Smiley (a character from *Saturday Night Live* in the early 1990s—google it) and tell yourself you are good enough. One of his best known quotes (as he would stare at himself in the mirror) was, "I'm good enough, I'm smart enough, and doggone it, people like me." The skit was called "Daily Affirmations with Stuart Smiley." What can you take from this? Tell yourself you're good enough. Talk yourself through the hard days—the better days are always just around the corner. This is something you can pull out of your bag of tricks any time you feel down.

2. All too often we tend to focus on the negatives—our flaws rather than our strengths. Make a list of all of the things that are good about you. If you have a hard time, ask a trusted friend or family member to help you. I once had a client have five friends write a list for her of all of the things they liked about her. She read them in a session with tears rolling down her face. She had no clue that others in her life had such positive things to say about her. This isn't to turn the focus to what others think about you instead of your opinion, but it can be a way to kick start your own thought process.

3. Reconnect with your body through some sort of physical activity. Research shows that people who engage in some form of exercise have more positive self-esteem than those who don't. This is not about running a marathon or being uber skinny. It's about finding physical activity that resonates with you (and lets you burn some of that negative energy) and then finding the fun in it.

4. For some reason, we as a people tend to attribute our successes to things outside our control (i.e., "It was easy" or "I got lucky") and our failures as being our fault (i.e., "I'm not smart enough" or "I'm not good enough"). This takes practice, but work to change these attributions. The idea that "I did well on my math test because it was easy" can be changed to "I did well on my math test because I'm smart and I studied hard."

5. Give yourself a boost each day. This can be taking time to listen to music that inspires you, engaging in an enjoyable activity, wearing a special outfit, or whatever makes you feel good. Try to find time to fit in one thing every day that makes you happy and makes you feel good.

6. Set goals for yourself and celebrate their attainment. Identify something that you want and then break it down into manageable pieces. An example might be: Clara has the goal of becoming a better tennis player. She may break this goal down into the following steps: improve her overall stamina, increase her service percentage, and improve her forehand returns. Clara then assigns tasks to each goal—how she's going to meet her goals, for instance, and running to improve her overall stamina. Each effort and related improvement is celebrated and acknowledged. Goals are something that we'll discuss further in chapter 3.

Chapter 2

RELATIONSHIPS

*Being with others
and still liking yourself*

~~~~~~~~~~~~~~~~~~~~~~~~~~~~

Y ou're in relationships with a number of people at any given time. You're in relationships with your friends and family, boyfriends and girlfriends, teachers and bosses, and everyone else with whom you interact. Some of these relationships are amazing, while others are terrible, and many bounce back and forth between these two extremes. Build on the lessons from the previous chapter, because a healthy self-esteem can only help you to build healthy relationships. If you feel bad about yourself, you're more likely to treat yourself badly and to allow others to treat you badly. You may feel unworthy of being treated well and you can't do any better than to be in relationships where people treat you like crap. This may happen, not just in dating relationships, but also in friendships and other relationships.

The opposite can be true too. If someone thinks too much of themselves, they may have unrealistic expectations about how others should treat them. They might have the belief that people in their lives should cater to them and always give them their way. They may believe that others are lucky to be dating them or to be their friend, which can cause them to treat others unfairly and unkindly. In relationships, as in many other areas of your life, the important factor is balance. It's important to feel good enough about yourself that you won't allow others to abuse you or treat you badly, but grounded enough to recognize that you shouldn't treat others poorly either.

I once had a client who was struggling with issues related to self-esteem and she didn't feel she deserved to have others be nice to her. So what happened? She gravitated to people who weren't nice to her, which only confirmed her belief that she didn't deserve kindness. We teach other people how to treat us. If you allow them to treat you like crap, certain people will be more than happy to treat you like crap. Everyone is to blame in this dynamic. Show people you want to be treated well. Call them on it if they're unkind. You don't have to be a bully who yells at everyone, just calmly explain that their behavior is unacceptable.

Get super comfortable in your own skin. Other girls being mean comes from THEIR insecurity and shouldn't feed yours.

Carrie Wilkerson—mentor, coach, advisor, and the Barefoot Executive

All too often someone who's giving you a hard time can appear strong and confident. This is so rarely the case! Someone who feels good about themselves has no need to try to make you feel small and insignificant. They're able to celebrate your successes and support you in your disappointments. Remember this from both sides. If someone is "torturing" you and appears to enjoy making your life miserable, that person is insecure and feels bad about herself. They're going after you in a feeble attempt to make them feel better, and that is a sad place for them to be.

I also want you to remember this if you ever find yourself in the position of the torturer. If you find yourself going after someone and making their life difficult for no apparent reason, ask yourself a couple of questions: What is it about this person that threatens me so much? Why is it so uncomfortable for me to let them be themselves? Adolescence is a period of exploration where people are trying to figure out what they believe and how they perceive the world.

Having someone who conflicts with your views can feel threatening. Let me give you an example: consider teens who focus on academics in high school vs. those who focus more on social opportunities. Each may think the other is wasting their time and may view them negatively. The root of this, though, is often fear. Seeing someone who is so different from you can cause you to fear that you're doing it wrong and making bad choices. That fear can cause you to behave rudely and disrespectfully. If, after some soul-searching, you recognize you were wrong, acknowledge it, ideally apologize, and go forward making different choices.

I know this happened to me all the time during my teen years. I'd feel terrible when my friends achieved successes, whether that success was in the form of great grades, a date with a hot guy, a great job, or triumphs in sports. I'd find myself trying to downplay what they had achieved as if their successes somehow highlighted my own failures, even when I wasn't in direct competition with them at the time. I wish I could say that it is something that I have magically outgrown in adulthood, but, sadly, I haven't. I still find myself wanting to compete, whether directly through myself or indirectly, like through my daughter. I'll hear that a friend's child is doing well at something (like playing piano) and my gut reaction is to start thinking about how I should sign my daughter up for piano lessons so she can be good at this too. When you feel the green-eyed monster creeping in, give yourself a shake and remind yourself that your friends' successes aren't your failures. You must be fairly amazing to have such amazing and talented friends. Clap for them and they'll be more likely to applaud you when your turn in the spotlight comes.

Surround yourself with people who want the same things for you that you do for yourself. We all need a cheering section.

Cindi Leive—editor-in-chief of *Glamour* magazine

This is about surrounding yourself with people who want you to succeed—whether that's getting into a good college or landing a date with your crush. They should behave in ways that support your dreams. A friend who knows your dream is to get into a good college won't encourage you to skip classes or blow off exams. She won't flirt with the guy you like or sabotage your tryout for the swim team. You need to be this friend for her as well as for yourself. You need to be the best possible friend you can be for you.

This is such a reciprocal process. You need your friends to be your cheering section, but you also need to be a part of your friends' cheering section too! Your friends will be better able to be cheerleaders for you when you can do the same for them. Go to their plays, competitions, and events and scream for them at the top of your lungs. Celebrate with them when they win—it's your success as well! You must be pretty damn special to have such talented and accomplished friends.

What about you and your achievements? Your friends should be hoisting you up on their shoulders and throwing you victory parades. This all depends on whether you choose to be friends with those people who are comfortable enough in their own skin to be able to support and congratulate your accomplishments. This is important in intimate relationships as well. I saw way too many relationships in high school where the guy would try to make the girl feel like crud so she would never think about breaking up with him.

A friend of mine dated a guy who was always criticizing her—she wasn't that pretty or smart, was gaining weight, and no other guy would ever want her. At that time, I was confused about why he wanted to date someone who he thought so little of. Why would anyone want to date someone who they thought was ugly, stupid, fat, and undesirable? Now, I know—the opposite was true. He was so insecure and felt so bad about himself that he didn't feel confident in his ability to keep her, so he tried to tear her down. He wanted her to feel so bad about herself that she would feel incapable of finding someone else if this relationship ended. She wouldn't dare leave him. His goal was to crush her self-esteem to the point that she would never leave him. People who love and value you will want to build you up, not break you down. Anyone who tells you you're not good enough is toxic to you.

You Are a Work of Art

I think my mom didn't want to share about sex because she thought it would make me go out and have sex. I'm pretty clear she wasn't ENJOYING glorious honoring blissful sacred sex with my Dad, so how could she tell me what was possible? What's the most tragic to me is that most moms don't understand the true FOUNDATION of sex ... which is sexual energy ... Sexual energy is the most powerful foundational energy of the Universe. Its life force energy is sexual energy. Birth. Life. Creation. What creates the trees, the bees, the artistic masterpieces ... and YOU ... yes YOU were created from sexual energy! This misunderstood energy is often placed in a taboo back drawer, and it is not embraced to be the very energy that makes you feel alive, honoring, caring, and tender with yourself and friends. It's also the energy that makes you feel vibrant, radiant, creative, and able to create masterpieces without using your analytical mind. It's also the energy that is orgasmic when you fully allow pleasure when the sun beats down on your skin, the breeze kisses your cheeks, the chocolate melts in your mouth, the sound of an incredible song gives you shivers, and one day if not already ... when your body experiences a sacred moment of Oneness with All that Is in sexual orgasm.

The advice that I wish was given to me is that sexual energy isn't just for the bedroom. It's 24/7 in all areas of experiencing joy, tenderness and pleasure. Its life affirming and feels like confidence. It's attractive to men, so know they will go bonkers. (You'll turn heads when you enter a room ... this is your potency not to be used as a manipulation, rather an inspiration for their most noble self to emerge.) Remember your body is a divine temple, a work of art to be honored, respected, cherished and adored ... worshipped. And with young men's hormones racing, it's OK to wait for a young man to truly treat you like the Priestess you are. For when you do decide to have sexual relations ... you get to choose to be honored like a work of art or used like a piece of meat. You create your standards. No games.

Just an open vulnerable and potent aware heart ... trust your knowing. Trust Your Knowing. You KNOW. You KNOW what feels expansive and what feels contractive. Your BODY knows if he's honoring of you, to use contraceptives, to enjoy kind joyous pleasure ... or to pass. Let the opinions of others fade away...even what I'm writing right now ... If it doesn't resonate, turn the page! Your knowing will never steer you wrong ... and your openness to Being and Dancing Alive AS the energy of the Universe, as Life Force Energy, as Sexual Energy ... will allow this Knowing, your birthright of Intuition, to guide you like a best friend your whole life long. You are magnificent!!!! Got it? (smile)

Allana Pratt—intimacy expert, author, host, speaker, advocate to end sexual violence

OK—wow, that was a lot of information. There's so much in these two paragraphs that I'm not really sure where to begin. I find myself wanting to avoid all discussion of sex because I don't want to say the wrong thing. I don't want to deny that many of you are sexually active, but at the same time, I don't want to encourage promiscuity. I think it would be naïve of me not to acknowledge that sex and sexuality are part of your everyday life. You may or may not be in a physical relationship with another person at this time, but your sexuality is always present, and it's important to remember that YOU are in charge of it. Everyone chooses how to display their sexuality; some put it on display front and center, while others choose to keep it private. Most are probably somewhere in the middle.

There's no right or wrong approach to this, but there are potential consequences associated with these choices. Unfortunately, others will often make assumptions about you based on how you present your sexuality—they may assume you're promiscuous because you're comfortable and confident in your sexuality or that you're "frigid" or a prude because you protect and guard your sexuality. You'll receive a lot of attention for putting your sexuality on display, which can be very flattering. Just be careful and make sure that you're doing what is right and comfortable for you and not just what other people want you to do.

The world is going to make certain assumptions about you based on the way you present yourself. One of these ways is the style in which you dress. It's not always so clear cut that if you're in a revealing outfit, you're a slut and if you're all covered up, you're a prude, but some of that certainly happens. It can go so much deeper than that. People who expose a lot of skin can be perceived as desperate and attention seeking. I'm all in favor of looking sexy (when appropriate), but remember there's a fine line between looking sexy and skanky. A little can go a long way. You might want to leave a little to the imagination.

Now, about sex. Many of you will choose to be involved in sexual relationships. What you need to make sure of is that you're doing so because you want to do so. You want to make sure that you're being valued and appreciated in these relationships. Your partner should feel grateful for the opportunity to be in your life. These positives should continue beyond the sexual act.

When I was in high school, my mom made a crack about how it was nice to be "wanted" but not always so great to be "had." I've had a number of girls in my practice who have slept with guys who had been giving them a lot of attention. They were caught up in the power of feeling wanted and desired. Unfortunately, what often happens is the guy gets his rocks off and once the act is complete, he moves on, leaving the girl feeling embarrassed and used. Choose wisely and remember that no one can value you if you don't value yourself. Value yourself—respect yourself enough to demand that others treat you with respect. Plenty of girls choose to have casual sexual relationships with various partners. This makes me a wee bit nervous. Just be careful. There are still a number of diseases out there that'll stick with you forever. You also don't want to regret treating sex so casually.

Hollywood has produced a number of movies where casual sexual relationships between friends develop into soul mate-type love affairs (i.e., *No Strings Attached* and *Friends with Benefits*). I'm sure this can happen in the real world sometimes; I just haven't seen it in my practice. What I typically see is that one person begins to have stronger feelings than the other and gets "attached." Someone ends up with hurt feelings and, often, the friendship is torpedoed. Take care and recognize what you're risking.

Everyone's a jerk until college. Bide your time. Get good at one thing.

Lisa Ann Walters—actress, comedienne, writer, film producer

This cracked me up, mostly because of the thread of truth that runs through it. In high school, many people are so angst-ridden that they can't hold it together long enough to consider anyone else's feelings. Part of this is developmental. It's called secondary egocentrism, which basically means that teens are often so focused on themselves that they struggle to understand that others might think or feel something different than they do. This makes it really hard to empathize with and be kind to others, since they can't get out of their own way.

The level of self-absorption gets a little better over the college years as people age and mature. I'm not sure if it is getting out of the petri dish of high school and into the larger environment of college (or job market), or it's simple aging and maturation, but these years have the potential for major growth. In college you get to pick your friends from the thousands who attend your school. I went to a very small high school (roughly 600 kids in grades nine to twelve) and, therefore, we had limited choices in our peer groups. Everyone knew everyone else and everything about their history. I then went to a large university with 40,000 to 50,000 students and had tons of people both similar to and different from me. I could select people who were a good fit for me and who challenged me to grow and develop. There were enough people around that I could mostly avoid those who I wasn't particularly fond of.

What should you do if you don't exactly love the social situation in high school? Listen to Lisa Ann Walters and "bide your time." High school, though it seems to last forever, is time limited. There is most definitely a light at the end of the tunnel.

Find a way to make the best of a bad situation—seek out support where you can find it, seek out hobbies and interests to build connections, and try not to take it personally when someone else's angst washes over you.

You've heard the phrase "It gets better" promoted to LGBT (lesbian, gay, bisexual and transgender) teens to help prevent suicidal behavior. That same phrase applies to us all. If high school is terrible, wait it out; it will get better, and you just need to give it a chance to improve. Know that you can get out and move on. You can move away from your parents and/ or classmates, if these relationships are toxic to you. No one can make you continue a relationship once you've made it to adulthood. Just get yourself there.

> What makes you angry in another may very well dwell within you. Check the mirror first and you'll find loving others easier.
>
> **AnnaLynne McCord**—actress

This is hard to do. I mean REALLY hard. All too often I hear girls bagging on each other for things they themselves also do—for instance, gossiping, hooking up with random guys, or being mean to each other. Frequently, we turn on each other and start tearing one another down rather than recognizing we're equally guilty of similar behaviors. Girls are so incredibly hard on each other! We hold each other to such impossibly high standards and then rip each other apart when we fail to live up to them. I'm not sure how this dynamic was set into motion, but it sucks. Tearing others down doesn't lift you up, in fact, often the opposite is true. Take a deep breath, take a step back, and calm yourself enough so that you can think clearly.

This reminds me of a story about my daughter, Charlie. Now she's only eight years old, but the example is still worth giving. Charlie came home from school one day and told me she no longer liked one of the girls from her class because the girl was bossy. We had a long talk about how to handle a bossy friend and even role-played how she should handle it the next time the bossiness occurred. I was feeling really confident in how I handled the situation (gave myself a "You are an awesome mom" pat on the back) and felt I had better prepared my daughter for life in the real world. Only after this extended period of self-congratulation, did I think to ask exactly what had happened between her and this other little girl.

Imagine my surprise when Charlie explained that this girl had refused to do what my daughter told her to do and THAT made the OTHER girl bossy. Sheesh! I had to swing that conversation around and explore my own daughter's bossiness and whether it's OK to expect other people to do what she tells them to do. I even threw in one my most hated sayings, "It's a pot calling the kettle black." I hated when my mom threw sayings like that at me as a kid, and it managed to lead to a ten-minute conversation with Charlie about which pot and what the heck is a kettle. But the saying is still true. Be careful that you're not blaming others for something you've done too. Try not to complain about someone else's gossiping as you are gossiping about her to your friends. Try not to call a girl a "slut" just for liking the same guy you're into.

I've also noticed that we can project our feelings onto others. I say that as I sit here in a grumpy mood. I realized, as I looked around at home and at the dance studio, that I was wondering why everyone else was in such a bad mood. I was really irritated that they were all being so negative. Oh…wait…that was me. I'm looking at them all through my Miss Grumpy Pants glasses. Take care not to assume others are feeling the same way you do.

Learn how to cope with difficult people in high school because you'll have to deal with these types for the rest of your life!

Hillary Kerr—editorial director
and co-founder of WhoWhatWear

Difficult people will surround you all the days of your life. They may be classmates or teachers in high school, your parents or friends, a boss or coworker when you are older. The role they may play in your life will vary, but the only guarantee is they will definitely be there. The challenge is figuring out how to interact with these people in a way to meet your goals without feeling like you're selling your soul to the devil.

I remember in middle school I had a teacher (I will not name him to be kind—see I can learn!) who was mean. He was really, really mean. He taught eighth or ninth grade geometry. He made fun of most of the students in the class and made us feel stupid, even though we were considered "advanced" by the school. He seemed to take an evil pleasure in making us feel bad about ourselves. Well, I decided I was going to teach him a lesson and began a silent protest.

I turned in every test blank and never completed a homework assignment the entire second semester of the school year. I thought I was flipping him the bird, and I was sure he was spending countless hours in frustration because he couldn't make me work. Not surprisingly I received an F that semester, and he never said a word about it. It wasn't until years later that I realized just how empty my protest was. I'd been blinded by righteous indignation. He wasn't upset that I was turning my assignments in blank, he was probably happy to have one less assignment to grade. My best revenge against him would've been to ace his class and move on and forget him (as I'm sure he forgot me the moment I walked out of the room).

A skill that I still need to master is to remember the power of your voice. Now, many may take this as a call for activism—to speak up for what is right, but this isn't how I mean it. What I need(ed) was to learn about the impact my words can have on others and to choose my words more carefully. When I was in high school, I was full of my own opinions and convinced in the rightness of those opinions. I was free with the expression of those opinions, often at the expense of others. I would've defended myself at the time, because I was only expressing my feelings and "telling the truth." Not all truths need to be shared. I wish I could've r learned to consider my audience sooner and contemplate my goals before speaking. Does this mean that I should've sat quietly and not spoken up? Of course not. But I was often my own enemy. I sabotaged my efforts by alienating those to whom I was speaking.

It's important to take those few moments and consider your goals. Think about who you'll be speaking to and how to say it in a way that might make it easier for them to agree with you. (Yes, this is a little bit of manipulation—so sue me). It reminds me of that old saying, "You can catch more flies with honey than vinegar." Yes, another one of "those" sayings. This is definitely true, but we need to not be shrinking violets either.

Sometimes in considering your audience, you may realize that they'll respond better to (or need) some backbone on your part. I guess what I'm saying is to choose your approach based on the audience and goals. You can't have one style of interacting with everyone and everything. Oh crap another saying, "Choose your battles." Remember you teach others how to treat you. If you allow people to walk all over you, there are people who will happily do so. If you allow boyfriends or girlfriends to disrespect you, some will happily do so.

Stick together.

Eliza Dushku—actress

Short and sweet, just like me. OK, I am short...There's power in numbers, and you have power through your relationships with others, whether they're friends or family. We all need a support system that we can rely on to help us through the hard times; one that will applaud us during our triumphs. Your support system will call you on it when you're out of line, but will not turn its back on you because of it.

Your support system will help you get your head on straight so you won't make the same mistake twice. It will not abandon you when it seems as though nothing is going right for you; instead, it will help you problem solve about what the heck to do next. You'll need to do the same for those in your support system. It's definitely not easy. It's often easier to walk away, but try not to ditch each other. Try not to turn on each other when things get hard. Make each other stronger rather than tearing each other down. You're only made stronger in your support of one another.

I'm so tired of hearing about "girl drama." There's almost an expectation that you will happily carve each other up to get ahead. This is total B.S. You're stronger than that! If someone falls on her face, offer her a hand. Few things feel worse than being alone after making a mistake.

Guidelines for healthy relationships:

1. **Communication**: An important part of any healthy relationship is open communication. You need to be able to share what you're thinking and feeling with friends, partners, and family. Your relationship should be a safe place for this exchange. You have an active part in this communication. Not only do you need to be open to hearing what others have to say to you, but you also need to make sure that the way you share things will help others listen to you. Take a moment to collect your thoughts and choose your words carefully. When you're yelling, your words are rarely heard by the other person—they just hear volume and noise.

2. **Respect**: Value your friends, family, and partners in the same way that you want them to value you. You demonstrate respect through your words and your actions. Be thoughtful and considerate of how

they think and feel. Treat them with admiration and deference.

3. **Balance**: The give and take in a relationship. Balance in a relationship has to do with fairness and whether each person feels that things are equal or not. It's very rare for a relationship to be 100 percent balanced at any given time. You may have a friend going through a horrible breakup, so for a period of time she may be needy, and you may be giving a lot of your time and energy to her. At this moment, the relationship is out of balance, and you're giving more to her and she is taking more. We need to look at the relationship as a whole. She may give to you during your struggles as well, and there may be balance across the relationship. Neither party should feel that they "always" have to be the giver as this only creates anger and resentment.

4. **Outside Interests**: There should be more in your lives besides each other. You should have other friends, family, hobbies, and interests. This isn't just true in dating relationships but in friendships too. This is important to your relationship, but it's also important for you as an individual. You're more than your relationship with any one person. You need to know there's more to you than this relationship, or you may be willing to accept being treated poorly in order to hold onto it.

5. **Conflict Resolution**: A healthy relationship is one where the people involved can work through their difficulties without attacking one another verbally or

physically. Yes, you will have arguments and that's OK, but conflict resolution involves open communication about different views followed by negotiation toward a peaceful conclusion. Does this mean you will always agree at the end? Nope—but the conclusion is one both parties feel they can live with without too much frustration or resentment.

6. **Forgiveness**: Gah! This one is hard! Healthy relationships need to have room for forgiveness. Everyone in a relationship is going to make mistakes. Guaranteed. Others need to be able to find a way to forgive those mistakes if the relationship is going to continue. Every person has identified "deal breakers" in their relationships—the things they can't forgive (i.e., infidelity, abuse, or dishonesty). That's 100 percent OK, but it's unhealthy for you to remain in a relationship where a deal breaker has occurred that you can't forgive. In those situations, it may be healthier to let go and move on.

7. **Fun**: You should enjoy being in your relationships! Find those things you can enjoy doing together—yes, even in your relationships with your parents!

8. **Supportive**: People with whom you have formed close relationships should be your loudest cheerleaders. They should want you to succeed, maybe even more than you want it yourself. You need to do the same thing for them. Their success is your success. You must be pretty damn amazing to have such amazing and talented friends.

9. **Affection**: This can be physical, verbal, or just "understood." A healthy relationship is one where you know the other people care about you. They genuinely like or love you just for being you. This may be stated or unstated, but you should know that it's there and you should be able to rely on it. When I got into trouble as a kid, my mom would say, "I still love you but I don't really like you right now." This may sound harsh, but it was comforting to me. It meant that no matter how big of a booger I might have been (and I was capable of epic boogerness), her love was never in jeopardy.

10. **Trust**: A healthy relationship can't exist without a solid foundation of trust. You need to know this person has your best interest at heart. They won't spill your secrets to others with the intention of hurting you. They won't cheat on you the second your back is turned. If you don't trust your partner (friend, parent, boyfriend, or girlfriend), it's important to take a moment to consider whether you have cause to doubt them. If so, consider whether this relationship is a good one for you to be in. If not, think about why you find it hard to believe in them. Is your own insecurity clouding your judgment?

11. **Acceptance**: A person in a healthy relationship likes you just for being you. They shouldn't be trying to get you to be smarter, or prettier, or funnier, or anything else. All too often I watched friends being changed by boyfriends in high school. Their boyfriends tried to choose their friends, activities, and even how they dressed. This typically seemed more about the boy's

insecurity than anything else. No one should have to change you in order to like you or accept you.

12. **Never, Ever Abusive**: None of the previous eleven items matter as much as this one. A healthy relationship is NEVER abusive—this means verbally, physically, sexually, or psychologically. Remember the deal breakers discussed in the forgiveness section? Abuse needs to be a deal breaker. A healthy relationship isn't one where anyone hits each other or makes each other feel "less than" or uses threats to control the other. It's important to note: Abuse is NEVER your fault. It's ALWAYS the abuser's fault. You should ALWAYS tell someone and ask for help. Remember, it's unusual for a person to become less abusive over the course of a relationship; rather, it usually escalates, often leading to serious injury and/or death. Pull others in to help you with this if you need it. Ending an abusive relationship can frequently be dangerous. Don't be embarrassed to ask for help. This isn't your fault. You deserve to be protected.

Chapter 3

GOALS

Deciding what the heck to do next and making it happen

~~~~~~~~~~~~~~~~~~~~~~~~~~~~~~~~

O K, what the heck are goals and how do you use them? Simple—you set goals all the time, even if you don't realize it. A goal is when you identify something you want and begin to make plans on how to get it. These goals can be short term, which means they can be accomplished in a short period of time (duh!). An example of a short term goal might be getting a good grade on your math test that's scheduled for Friday. Your plan? Study! A long term goal is one that needs to take place over a longer period of time (double duh!).

A long term goal might be going to a good college. The plan would include making decisions based on that goal as far back as freshman year (i.e., signing up for extracurricular activities, studying for good grades, etc.). I was the queen of long term goals. It's a joke in my family that my mom stood over my crib chanting, "College...college...college" when I was just a baby. Talk about a long term goal! I always made fun of her for it, but I find myself doing the same thing with Charlie. Poor thing chose Stanford as her college of choice when she was four years old—no pressure! Hey, if she can get in—more credit to her!

A client recently gave me an analogy about motorcycle riding that I think applies really well here. He told me when you ride a motorcycle you can't just look at what's right in front of your tire because everything else that comes along will be a surprise to you. He told me that you also have to be looking into the distance so you can see what's coming from further out. Life is like this. You need to be watching (and preparing) for what's coming up soon, but you also have to keep an eye out for those things that are a little further out as well. Your front tire is your short term goals, but looking out into the distance is your long term goals.

You might ask yourself why it's important to set goals. Well, to know where the heck you're going! If school is important to you, then you likely have a lot of goals related to school. The same thing applies to hobbies, sports, and other interests. We set goals for those things that are most important to us. When you set goals, you can identify the steps necessary to reach your goal. It identifies the path you need to follow.

You have to find a goal in life and never take your eyes off of it. I started to study in high school after my science teacher got me interested in science. You have to work hard over a sustained period to achieve and be successful. High school was difficult for me. I was teased and bullied. Keeping my eyes on my goal of becoming a scientist kept me going.

Temple Grandin—doctor of animal science and professor at Colorado State University, bestselling author, autism activist, and consultant to the Livestock Industry on Animal Behavior

Temple Grandin is a genius! Goals can be self-protective, especially if you're having a not-so-great high school (or current life) experience. Take a deep breath and remind yourself that this time in your life can be limited. The knowledge that there's a light at the end of the tunnel can make the wait more bearable. Thinking about how your post-high school life or college life will be different may help to get you through current challenges.

When you're struggling, it may seem like things are never going to change, never get better. If you start to plan for your future, it can help remind you that this time is temporary, as are its hardships. Having something to look forward to can give you hope. Start planning for that life—get the grades to get you into the college of your choice, think about financial aid options, and/or pad your high school transcripts with those highly desirable extracurricular activities.

This can apply to many situations. If you have a difficult home life, remember this is time limited as well. Once you graduate from high school, your options become much more plentiful. You can move out of your parents' house, get a job, go to college, leave town, enlist in the military, and so many other things. Consider where you want to end up and begin plotting out what to do in order to get there. I've had clients who are miserable living at home with their parents—whether with good reason or not.

I often discuss coping strategies with them to use until they can get out. This involves setting goals to make escape possible—do you need to get into college, find a job, or save money? It involves keeping yourself mentally strong enough not to be "destroyed" by the time remaining in the environment (home, school, wherever). Most importantly, we talk about not doing anything that would make your escape impossible—suicide, criminal activity, drug abuse, etc. You want to make sure when the time comes to go, you're able to go.

A key point not to be overlooked is the importance of hard work in reaching your goals. Few of the things in life that matter are easy. You'll have to commit time and energy to your goals. You'll have to pick yourself back up when you stumble and keep trying until it works. Most goals require hard work over a considerable period of time. I can hear my mother saying, "Nothing important comes easily."

It will be up to you to decide which of your goals are worth working for and how long you're willing to work to reach them. A good support system can help you keep working, even when it gets really hard. Find people who are willing to be your cheerleaders to keep you going, even when you might want to give up. These can be teachers, family members, friends, counselors, clergy members, coworkers, and/or teammates.

They're anyone who will keep pushing you forward, even when you want to throw in the towel.

> When I decided to run for public office, there were people in my life to whom I was very close that didn't approve. This was difficult for me because I valued their opinions; however, I had the passion for public service and I knew in my heart it was what I wanted. My advice to young people is to believe in yourself and if people in your life don't agree with your goals, you need to stay strong and do what you think is right. Have confidence that you can achieve anything to which you set your mind. Although there will be many challenges you face during your lifetime, embrace them and learn, and don't be afraid to stand up for what you believe in, even if it isn't popular.
>
> **Mimi Walters**—Republican
> state senator from California

How should you handle it when your goals are not popular with others? These can be your friends or family, teachers and bosses, or anyone else with whom you interact. There's no easy answer to this, so I'll just say…it depends. I want to encourage you to consider the feedback you receive from the people in your life and take some time to think about whether there's a reason to be worried. If you tell me that your goal is to be the best drug dealer in town, I'm going to have concerns. I actually had a client tell me this once! He actually had a master plan on how to take over our town weed distribution and not get caught by the police.

If you were to tell me something similar, I'd want to talk with you about the physical and legal dangers of becoming a drug dealer. I may even tell you that I wouldn't be willing to spend time with you if this was your career path—because I wouldn't want to be confused for a druggie or caught in the middle of a drug deal gone wrong. I don't think I'd fare well in jail. You still have the right to choose this as your goal; others just may not want to be involved. Obviously this seems like a ridiculous example, but the point I want to make is you should consider the feedback of others and then make your own choices.

But, if you hear them out and really listen to their reasons and still feel that your goals are in your best interest, then keep going! Work hard! In some families there are expectations about what college you must attend, or career you should pursue, or sport you have to play. Your goals may deviate from these expectations. Consider the consequences and make your choice. Is your family the "disown you and never speak to you again" type or the "disappointed for a while but will get over it" type? Does this matter to you? Your friends can have similar expectations—you must participate in this activity, or you have to be friends with these people, or you need to earn these grades in order to be accepted.

Your goals may be different from those in the group—your jock friends may not like that you're in the school musical, for example (*High School Musical*, anyone? Can you tell I have an eight-year-old?). How can you manage when your goals don't match up to those in your group? You're the only one that can make this decision. What is more important to you—the goal or the acceptance of your group/family? It's incredibly hard to go against what others want/expect from you. I was as guilty of this as anyone else in high school—I twisted myself into knots trying to be accepted. I always looked at college as my chance to be free and to start doing the things that I wanted to do. Maybe you won't have to wait that long.

I desperately wanted a tattoo my sophomore year in college and was well aware my mom wasn't going to be a huge fan of the idea. Here's the thing—I was over eighteen and could, legally, tattoo myself to my heart's content. There was a kicker: my mom was paying for college. I didn't want to do anything to disrupt the gravy train. I had a choice, right? My choice—negotiation! I called my mom and asked for her permission. Lame, I know, but she relented with very specific conditions—smaller than the bottom of a Coke can and placed somewhere that it could be hidden in my post-college career. It's exactly the size of the bottom of a soda can and is hidden behind my right shoulder. Side note—if you ever plan on getting a tattoo, think long and hard before you choose what to get. Mine is lame, and I wish I'd selected something more personally meaningful.

What if your goal is to be happy and this feels like it's in direct conflict with what others in your life want? What if it feels like it's impossible to have what you want and they want at the same time? Over the course of my practice, I've had a number of teenage clients who have been struggling with their sexual orientation and fears that they'll (at best) disappoint their parents or (at worst) be disowned and "damned to eternal hell fire" because they're gay or lesbian. I've never been able to tell these teens what they should do because it's not my decision to make. I offer support and validation and discuss with them their concerns that their families may reject them (which they might). We talk about the importance of being happy and being able to accept who they are as individuals. Sometimes the fear of telling others that we're different from what they expect is also the fear of accepting the same thing about ourselves. Whether you're gay or straight, want to play tennis or not, want to attend your mother's alma mater or somewhere else—you have to accept your own differences before you can begin to ask others to do the same.

> Be unafraid. I'm proof even impossible dreams can come true. So shift into drive and go fast after what makes you happy.
>
> **Ann Curry**—television personality, news journalist, photojournalist

I recently had a client tell me that setting goals was too overwhelming. She thought that once she set a goal, she was expected to know all of the steps to reach that goal and to have the plan solidly in place. Holy crap! Talk about pressure! Identifying your goal is the first step, and you aren't expected to already know the tenth step. Figure out what you want—start laying out the steps to get there and figure it out as you go.

Once you have identified your goals, it's time to start working toward them. This involves a certain amount of bravery—if you're going to TRY, you have to risk FAILURE. The possibility of failure is scary, scary business, but the payoff can be amazing.

Dream big! You have your whole life ahead of you and now IS the time to dream big. If you want to be a doctor, start studying. If you want to be an actress, start auditioning. If you want to be a professional athlete, start practicing. Backup plans are always a good idea—I love a good safety net. You want to make sure that you have something to fall back on in case the big dream doesn't happen. Get an education (college or vocational) and know that you'll be able to take care of yourself. Find what makes you happy and focus your energies on getting to do that as often as possible.

The advice I wish I had heard from someone when I was young is that you are important. People will always push you to do things they think are important, but those things might not be right for you. Your wants, needs, ideas, self are valuable and important, and should never be disregarded. When I was young, I spent a lot of time listening to others and disregarding my own wants and needs. I thought it was better to make others happy than myself. This led me to become very unhappy, and initiated a cycle of self-negation that was very hard to break out of. Over the years, I did eventually break the cycle, and now I work very hard to listen to and heed the inner voice that is my true self. I am much happier and am living the life I want to live.

Kiki Sanford—science communicator

You're important. Let me say that one more time; you're important. You have the right to pursue things that make you happy. You matter. Your wants, needs, and interests are just as important as those of anyone else. People who love and support you should try to help you reach your goals and should get out of the way when your momentum is pushing your forward. I participated in a couple of school plays in high school. Drama was not a popular activity at the time and I knew it wasn't well respected among my friends. None of my friends ever told me to quit or even made fun of it, but I still allowed what they thought to color my enjoyment.

During my senior year, the director offered me the lead in the play. I found I couldn't tolerate such an attention-grabbing role given my mixed feelings about drama as a whole and quit all together. If I'd felt more supported, maybe I would've stuck with it—I'm not sure. You can't always blame all of the interference you face on them, though. Sometimes it's your fault. You might be letting other people get in your way— either because you aren't confident in your plans or because you're afraid of success. No one made me quit the school play; I did that all on my own.

Fear of success is a very real thing! Shocking, I know! You'd be amazed at how many times people act in self-sabotaging ways because they're terrified of what will happen once they reach their goals. Let's think of someone whose goal it is to get into college. They might find themselves pushing along and almost there when the anxiety hits—*How am I going to pay for school? Where am I going to live? How will I move away from all of my friends? What if I hate everyone there? What if I can't hack it and flunk out?* These fears about what can happen once the goal has been reached can lead you to shoot yourself in the foot.

You may stop doing your homework or studying for exams. You may "accidentally" miss important college application deadlines. If you ever find yourself falling farther and farther away from your goals, give yourself a moment and take a deep breath. See if you aren't acting as your own worst enemy and, if you are, talk yourself back down off of the ledge. Take a deep breath and refocus your energies. You're an amazing creature, a force of nature. You can survive anything, even your own success.

How to set goals:

1. Figure out what the heck you want. This may seem like it should be the easy part, but it can be really challenging. Be as specific as you can possibly be so you can make your plan better. For instance the goal, "I want to get my biology grade up to a B" is clearer than "I want to get better grades." "I want to land my back layout" is clearer than "I want to be a better gymnast." The more specific you are, the easier it'll be for you to break down the steps needed to reach your goal and to recognize it when you get there.

2. If your goal is big, break it down into smaller, more manageable goals. These can be step-by-step instructions to reach your goal. For instance, if your goal is to make the tennis team, you may have a series of smaller goals designed to help you make the team. Your goals may include: running a 7-minute mile,

improving your first serve percentage, increasing the speed of your serve, and improving your overall rank. Your smaller goals may be gradual improvements you need to get you toward your ultimate goal. For instance, if your goal is to run a 7-minute mile and you're currently running a 10-minute mile, you may set specific goals such as running a 9:30 mile, then a 9:00 mile, then a 8:30 mile, and so on until you reach your final goal. There are tons of reasons to break down big goals, but the most important ones are the increased ability to track and reward your progress and to reduce feeling overwhelmed by the size of the bigger goals. If you were to focus on running a 7-minute mile when you're currently running a 10-minute mile, you may not believe it's even possible and give up before really trying.

3. Have different goals for different areas of your life so you can work on different things simultaneously. You may have goals for school and career development, family and home life, friends and social areas, physical areas, and mental and spiritual functioning. It's OK to have goals like getting a B in biology, running a 9-minute mile, and finding a part-time job all in place simultaneously. Progress toward your goals can be faster in some areas than in others—this is OK too! You may check off some goals (and make new ones) while others are still ongoing.

4. State your goal in positive terms. Changing the ways you state your goals can change how successful you

are in achieving them. It's better to state, "I'll make better food choices" instead of "I won't eat sugar." Both are focused on the same thing—healthier eating, but stating the goal more confidently can help you view it more positively too.

5. Write down your goals. Putting them down on paper makes them real and confirms your commitment. You can go back and reread them any time you need reminding. Keep your goals somewhere handy. Some people like to post their goals where they can readily see them (i.e., on the refrigerator or the bottom corner of the mirror), or you can have them somewhere easily accessible (i.e., in your notebook or wallet). It can also help to share your goals with others. If you goal is to quit smoking (you should never, never smoke in the first place), then telling others can help with accountability. Your friends who know you are trying to quit will call you on it if they see you lighting up.

6. Remind yourself about your goal. You can say it ten times each morning. You can check in with yourself frequently to determine if specific behaviors will help or hurt your chances of reaching your goal. Let's talk about the person whose goal it was to get a B in biology. If she is tempted to blow off an assignment, she may ask herself if ditching the paper will help or hurt her chances of reaching her goal of earning a B in biology.

I'm stealing an idea from Kim McSwain—she's on the faculty for Nuvo Dance Convention, and my daughter recently took one of her classes. Make a Dream Cloud for yourself. Cut a piece of paper into the shape of a cloud. Write your goals inside the cloud—whatever you're working on at the time. Tape this cloud where you'll see it every morning. When you wake up, read your goals and ask yourself what you're going to do that day to help you reach your goals. A little gimmicky, I know, but it sounded so awesome that I wanted to have one for myself!

7. Get off your butt! Start working on your goal. If you have a hard time beginning your goal, start using a reinforcement system. If it's a challenge to make yourself do your biology homework each night, set up a reward program. Think of small things you want and only give them to yourself when you get your homework done. For instance, watch an episode of a favorite TV show only if you complete your work. This might be the extra motivation you need to get you moving in the right direction. I made myself work on my dissertation (a disgustingly long paper) by bribing myself with gummy bears. Not the healthiest system by any means, but it got the job done.

8. Check in on your progress. How are you doing toward reaching your goal? It's OK to realize that you need to make changes along the way. If your current plan isn't working, reassess and make those changes that are needed to get there. Just keep working on it.

SMART System to Goal Setting

S—**Specific**: Be clear with what you want. "I want to run a 7-minute a mile" is more specific than "I want to be able to run faster."

M—**Measurable**: Have your goal be something that is measurable so you'll be able to assess your progress and know when you've reached your goal. "I want to earn a B in biology" vs. "I want to be a better student."

A—**Attainable**: Your goal needs to be something that you feel is within your reach. If you truly believe that you're at best a B student, then setting a goal of straight A's may be ridiculous. If you don't believe your goal is attainable, you may find it impossible to fully commit to the goal and you may be quick to give up. My goal could never be to play in the NBA—it's impossible in every way possible, so it's not an attainable goal for me, even if I do have a decent free throw shot.

R—**Realistic**: Let's not set ourselves up for failure and disappointment, OK? You want to make sure that your goal is possible. "I want to learn ten new Spanish words a week" is possible, while "I want to be fluent in Spanish in one week" isn't.

T—**Timely**: You need to set a realistic time frame so you have a clear target to aim toward. Goals that aren't anchored by a target date aren't taken seriously—there's no urgency. "I'll learn to throw an aerial" can happen at any time, which means I can procrastinate with the best of them—"I'll start tomorrow" or"…next week" or "…next month." Setting time limits can help to motivate you—"I'll land my aerial by June 1st" means that I need to get working in order to make that timeline.

Chapter 4

INSTINCTS

*Listening to that little voice
that tells you what to do*

~~~~~~~~~~~~~~~~~~~~~~~~~~~~~~

in·stinct ($\text{ĭn}'\text{stĭngkt}'$)

n.

1. An inborn pattern of behavior that is characteristic of a species and is often a response to specific environmental stimuli: *the spawning instinct in salmon; altruistic instincts in social animals.*

2. A powerful motivation or impulse.

3. An innate capability or aptitude: *an instinct for tact and diplomacy.*

Instinct [Def. 1, 2, & 3]. (n.). In American Heritage Dictionary of the English Language. (4th ed.). (2001). Boston, MA: Houghton, Mifflin, Harcourt.

Instincts are behaviors or impulses that exist without thought and are frequently innate or unlearned. They give direction in the decisions we make, often contributing to our basic survival. Your instincts may cause you to run out of a burning building or to move to the opposite side of the street because an oncoming stranger gives you the "willies." Those willies are your instincts—your gut telling you something's wrong. It's incredibly important (and often difficult) to listen to your instincts. These are the messages your body sends you to let you know if a situation is a good one for you or not. All too often we ignore our "gut feeling" and try to convince ourselves that everything's OK and that we're overreacting. I strongly advise you not to ignore your gut. Listen to that voice—it's trying to protect you.

There are a lot of theories about what instincts really are, but most seem to focus on the idea that instincts are created by the signals your brain picks up from your environment that you don't consciously notice—a shadow around the corner of the room just outside your normal field of vision, the way a person shifts their eyes as they share a story with you, or an unusual scent in the room that might stir a strong reaction in you. Something's telling you there might be a problem.

Most of our early instincts are related to survival. Early humans needed to trust their instincts for their immediate safety. Was there a predator nearby? Was the weather changing in such a way as to necessitate finding shelter? Ignoring these instincts could've led to serious injury or even death. You don't have to go back to prehistoric man to see the ways instincts function in our lives. Many animals are born with the capabilities of surviving without their mothers if that situation was to arise. This isn't the case for human babies. Without an older person available to see to their care, they'll quickly suffer and die. This is why they cry—to seek out the assistance of older humans. They cry because they're hungry, tired, and uncomfortable. No one teaches babies to do this. They're born with the instinct to cry when they need help. The cry is often so annoying that we will do almost anything to make it stop.

A few months ago, I was at the movies with my mom and daughter watching some G-rated cartoon. The theater was filled with parents and children enjoying entertainment that was approved for all ages. Once we sat down, I noticed a young man sitting all by himself two seats over from me. He was sitting with his hoodie pulled up and was scrunched down in his seat. This was a relatively short period of time after the movie theater shooting in Aurora, Colorado. Something about him made me uncomfortable—I'm not sure if it was because the shooting had just been in the news, or the fact that he was an adult alone in a children's movie, or if it was just a "vibe" or instinct. I found myself thinking that I should take my family and leave the theater.

I found myself watching him instead of the movie and plotting what I could do to protect my daughter if he proved to be dangerous. In the end, I did nothing. I watched him instead of the movie and nothing happened. Once we got home, I told my husband about what had happened and expected him to make fun of me for being "paranoid," but he didn't. He was mad. Really mad. What I got instead of being laughed at was a lecture about listening to my gut. He asked me an important question—what would I regret more: listening to my gut and leaving the movie theater unnecessarily or staying and having something horrible happen. Good question, huh?

Good question. Honor your gut. If you stop trusting it, it will abandon you and you will be lost...

Jennifer Carpenter—actress

Now that our lives aren't in peril on a daily basis (thank goodness), many of us have ignored or abandoned our instincts. We often feel we're being paranoid or ridiculous if we trust the feeling something is not OK. We worry about making a fool out of ourselves by overreacting. I would so much rather that you are embarrassed but safe than potentially seriously harmed in some way. If you ever get the feeling that something isn't quite right, listen to it. Take it seriously and consider it as one of the pieces of information you use to make your decisions.

Listen to Jennifer Carpenter. If you ignore your instincts long enough, you'll stop hearing them. Think of your instincts as a trusted friend. If your best friend were to try to talk to you over and over again about something and you ignored her, she would stop trying. Chances are she would throw her hands up in the air in disgust and frustration and start talking to someone who would listen to her. Your instincts work in much the same way—you listen to them and they get stronger, but ignore them and they'll fade away into silence. Remember your valued friend—you don't have to automatically do what she tells you to do without question, but you do need to hear her out and consider what she has to say. She may have something important to add that might make your decisions easier to make.

Follow your heart and intuition. It is always right! Don't second guess yourself! Listen to your instinct!

Vanna White—television personality, actress

Trust yourself. Your intuition is you. You're picking up something in your environment that's making your "spidey sense" tingle. Take a beat to think things over and look at the situation more closely. Consider whether or not what you're picking up is warranted and if you need to make a change based on it.

I enrolled at Michigan State University as an accounting major in my freshman year. I finished my first year in that program with a mediocre grade point average (GPA) and a lack of energy for my classes. My heart just wasn't in it. I was tempted to ignore the fact that changing my major to something I really enjoyed (psychology) would make me happier. I thought accounting would require a fewer number of years in school than a PhD in psychology (which it would have) and what I perceived as greater job security.

I finally realized that I was only making myself miserable. I was trying to ram a square peg (me) into a round hole (accounting). I just didn't like accounting and kept feeling pulled to psychology. I needed to listen to my heart, even if it meant I would have to go to school longer and I might earn less money. Unfortunately, it also meant the accounting and higher level math courses I'd already completed were reclassified as electives in my psychology program. No billiards or yoga classes for me.

Don't follow anyone else's advice! You will always know what you need, who are you if you listen to your heart!

Jena Malone—actress, musician

It's interesting that Jena Malone advised you not to listen to anyone's advice in a book filled with advice! Maybe she was being ironic. Beyond the possible irony, there's important information here. Ultimately, you need to be true to yourself. You're the only one who can determine the right next step for you. The biggest area of conflict I've seen is deciding what to do after college. There's often conflict between what others (teachers, parents, and friends) may want for you and what you want for yourself. You may all have different plans about how you should go about achieving your goals. As with any piece of advice, listen to what they have to say and then listen to your heart. If your parents want you to go to medical school and you faint at the sight of blood—this is probably a no go. If you want to move to New York City and become a professional musician, your parents may have a heart attack and fear for your future. Listen to their advice and then listen to your heart.

When it was time to apply to college, I had my heart set on studying abroad. Not just for a semester, but for the entire four years. You may not be surprised to learn that my mom was not excited about the idea. We discussed the idea and I realized she had a point—she was also paying for college! I realized I didn't want to leave the country enough to pay for it on my own, which was a very real possibility. I stayed in the U.S. and had a fantastic college experience anyway. Listen to their advice and then listen to your heart (and, unfortunately, sometimes also to your pocketbook).

Please, please, please apply this concept to peer pressure. Your friends are always going to have something to say about what you should and should not do. Listen to what they say and then check your gut. You can't simply do what others tell you to, rather you need to listen to your heart. If anyone ever tells you to do something that doesn't feel right to you, don't do it. Anyone, whose relationship with you is conditional on your doing what they want, is not necessarily worth the effort.

I had a friend in middle school who shoplifted like crazy. She took clothes, jewelry, shoes, makeup—it didn't matter if she "needed" it or not. Sometimes she had plenty of money on her to pay for what was stolen, but she got a rush from stealing. It didn't take long before she was pushing me to join in. It took me a little while, but I realized she wanted me to shoplift to make her feel better. If we were both doing it, it couldn't be that bad, right? She ended up getting caught and was arrested not too long later and ultimately changed schools.

"Friends" will often want you to share in their bad behavior (smoking, alcohol, sex), because it makes them feel better about their own behavior. Take care of yourself and try to avoid getting pulled into someone else's drama. This applies to friends, family and anyone else. I don't care if they're pressuring you to do drugs, have sex, not to have sex, or go to college. You need to listen to what they have to say, but then check in to see what feels right to you. Can you live with either decision? What are the consequences to your choices? If a choice makes you uncomfortable with its "wrongness"— there's your answer. If the potential consequences are too great, there's your answer.

Be unafraid of the unknown, be true to yourself, none of us are perfect but all of us are valuable!

Lisa Cochran Neilan—television producer

The unknown can be a scary place that many strive to avoid. This anxiety or fear can leave you frozen in the same place for way too long. Each new change that you make can be scary and unknown, but can also lead to something that's magnificent. The unknown doesn't always have to lead to a bad thing. I moved to California from Michigan by myself in my mid-twenties. I had enrolled in Pepperdine University for my doctorate and my boyfriend (now husband) still had a year left at Michigan State University. I don't mind admitting I was scared to death. I had never lived more than a couple of hours from my parents and had been at MSU for six years. I had no idea what to expect and didn't know a single person in California. I stumbled around a bit and fell on my face a few times, but it ended up being both a terrifying and amazing experience. We're still in California today. Stand up tall and take it on if it's something you really want.

But what if you try something new and it doesn't work out? What is that word? Gasp! Failure. (We'll talk more about this in chapter 7. It's a big enough issue that it deserves a chapter all to itself.) The important part to remember is that failure isn't the end of the world. You're not perfect. The world isn't perfect. You won't succeed at everything you attempt.

I contacted tons of people for this book and quite a few said, "No." Not just potential contributors, but also literary agents. The knowledge that this book would definitely receive rejection (a lot of rejection) before it could ever find a publisher could have stopped me from going forward. Think of all the things that wouldn't have been attempted if people gave in to their fears. If the biggest concern you have about trying something new is that it might not work—go for it! Whether it works out or not, remember that your value isn't decided by this decision alone. You're valuable whether you succeed or fail.

You will find your groove, the place where you think this is where I'm the best version of me.

Brooke K. Travis—director of luxury brands at Starwood Hotels

---

This is part of trusting yourself. If you keep working at finding what you want in life and how to get there, you'll figure it all out. I had to flounder around a bit in college—tried on a few majors until I found one that fit. Then I had to flounder around a bit in grad school while trying to figure out what I wanted to specialize in. Once I graduated, I had to flounder some more until I could figure out the best setting in which to work and how to make it fit the life that I wanted. Do I have it all figured out? Nope. Not a chance. But every now and then I need to flounder around in order to determine what the hell I want to do next.

Give yourself that chance. Sometimes you have to sit in the crap for a little while before you can settle on your next logical step. We're tempted to jump out of the crap as quickly as we can because it's uncomfortable (and smelly). Fight that temptation! Sometimes you need to sit in it to really decide where you want to go. Uncertainty is really uncomfortable, and we often think that any decision (even the wrong one) is better than uncertainty. This isn't always the case.

Give yourself a little more time to make your choices. I have a friend who's super reactive—everything is about "what's next?" Something happens to her and her immediate response is to jump into her next choice because being still is so uncomfortable to her. If she loses a job, she immediately begins applying for anything and everything because her automatic reaction is to get a new job as soon as possible. She can't give herself the time to think through job possibilities and focus her job seeking efforts in the direction she wants to take her career. This, unfortunately, can lead to a new job she doesn't enjoy or one that isn't a good fit for her. Be proactive rather than reactive. Think through the situations you're presented with and plan where you want to go next. You'll continue to have opportunities to improve every day of your life. You'll have opportunities to be your "best self" so many times, and each time you can be 100 percent confident in the belief that you've made the best decisions you could make for yourself at the time.

Rules to live by:

No naked pictures EVER!!! Unless you think your career path might be a Playboy model or porn star. Nothing good will ever come of it.

Never shave your legs or bikini line, wax.

Get your eyebrows shaped professionally. By someone who has great looking brows themselves.

Take off your make-up before bed.

Drink lots of water.

Smile.

When you're choosing a career, follow your dreams. Don't let people tell you that what you want to achieve isn't possible. Maybe you won't make it, but at least you'll have tried. And if you don't try, you'll never know what might have been.

Always ask for what you want in life, the worst you will hear is no; the yeses are amazing!

Have fun. You never know how much time you have on earth, so make the most of it.

Anne-Marie Sweeney—journalist, broadcaster

I love this! Let me start at the top of the list. First and foremost—no naked pictures ever. If you take one piece of advice from this book, *this is the one*. More often than not, these pictures will come back to bite you in your overexposed ass. No matter how much you think you can trust the person to whom you're sending the pictures too many things can go horribly wrong. Think Kim Kardashian here. I know she got a TV show out of the deal, but you really do not want your nether bits on display to the world.

You'll likely get into a fight with or breakup from anyone you date in high school. Relationships rarely end well at this age. Don't give this type of ammunition to anyone else to use against you. Particularly since your pictures will likely only be passed around your high school, and we all know how maturely high school students can handle these things....

Eyebrow shaping is important (no unibrows, please), but you can apply this across so many fields. I've never worked out with a trainer who wasn't in better shape than I am (not that it's too difficult to find someone who's fitter than I am, let me tell you). I always look at the hair of anyone who is going to mess with mine. If it looks like ass, they're not likely going to be able to do great things with my own mop.

At a store, I seek the advice of the salesperson who looks well put together, particularly if they have a look that I'm trying to achieve. When seeking out any advice, find an expert. Find someone who knows more than you do to point you in the right direction. Remember, this is only advice, not a command. Whatever you decide needs to feel right to you.

Wash your face—especially if you're wearing makeup, but even if you aren't. Take care of your skin. Use sunscreen and watch how much time you spend in the sun. You'll appreciate this as you get older. I'm far from good at this. I'm still learning. Drinking water is good for your skin, but it's also good for your whole body. Drinking water reduces the amount of soda and other crud you're drinking too.

Smiles are contagious. When you smile, neurochemicals in your brain are released that actually increase your overall feelings of happiness. People who are smiling are viewed as more approachable, likeable, and confident. Your smile will often be met with a smile in response.

Next—career. This is such a big topic that I've given it its own chapter. That's coming in chapter 5.

Asking for what you want is not just a suggestion, it's a necessity. If you don't tell people what you want, they won't have a clue. No one can read your mind (Thank the Lord—mine is a scary, scary place!) You never know, they just might say yes. Is it a guarantee? Hell no, but if no one knows what you want, it's almost a definite no.

Enjoy yourself. There are no guarantees in life, and you need to have your fun while you can. Have fun, but be safe and be smart.

~~~~~~

There's a lot in this world we have no control over, like other people's actions, whether or not some guy likes us, and tons about our appearance, to name a few. I remember hating how bony my wrists were, and crying over a guy who never called me when he said he was going to. It's easy to become obsessed over things we can't control. The good news is that some of the most important stuff, like our intelligence and personality, we *do* have some control over. This is the time to develop your smart and savvy side.

Being smarter means making better decisions in your life—everything from the career you choose to the friends (and guys) you choose to surround yourself with—and that will lead to a much happier life, trust me. And how do we *become* smarter? By challenging ourselves with things like mathematics. I'm not kidding. In fact, math is like going to the gym, for your brain! The more you do hard math problems and struggle through them, the stronger your brain gets, and the better problem solver you become—in all areas of life.

Danica McKellar—actress, NYT bestselling author
of *Math Doesn't Suck* and *Kiss My Math*

This can be a challenge for so many of us. There can be a great struggle in identifying those things that are within our area of control and those that aren't. If you keep trying to have some impact on those things that are outside your area of control, you'll only end up frustrated and disappointed. It's a waste of your energy. Examples of things outside your control are someone else's behaviors, thoughts or feelings, whether or not you're attracted to someone, your height (trust me on that one!), or the weather. What you can control, though, is your reactions to these things.

You can control the types of people with whom you surround yourself. You can control the types of situations in which you place yourself. By doing so, you can do what Danica recommends, and you can make yourself smarter. Choose wisely the people you allow into your life. Choose wisely where you go. Prepare and exercise your brain, as you do your body, and it will become stronger and better equipped to assist you in the future.

Strategies to hone your instincts:

1. Pay attention. All too often we ignore our gut reaction to situations in favor of logical, rational thought. We sit and make lists of pros and cons rather than listening to the little voice whispering yes or no. If you have a strong physical or emotional reaction to a situation, don't ignore it in favor of lists.

2. Look at times in your life when things turned out well. Did you trust your gut? Maybe it was having a "feeling" that a new friend couldn't be trusted. Or the decision to end a relationship. Or leaving a party when something told you things were about to go sideways. Whatever the situation, think about what the triggers were that told you something was wrong—where did you feel that in your body? Have you ever ignored that feeling in the past? How did that situation turn out?

3. Now take the next step. Look back at the times when things went to the crapper. Make a list of situations where you had a "feeling" and you ignored it. Ask yourself the same questions—what were you feeling and where were you feeling it? What could have been different if you had listened to your instincts? Use this information to remind you of the importance of listening to your instincts in the future.

4. Focus on face-to-face meetings. All too often we interact with people through email, text, or Twitter. Do you know what's missing from these interactions? Body language! This important piece of information is often missing in our communications. We're forced to assume how people feel. Don't fall for it. Talk in person and you may get a better feeling about who they are.

5. Make paying attention to your body a priority. This gives you permission to listen to your gut. Pay attention to how your body tells you there's a problem. When you're upset, do you get headaches, an upset stomach, or back pain? When these symptoms occur, pay attention! Something big could be going on.

6. Set a goal to achieve one small instinctive accomplishment each day. Whether you're deciding what shoes to wear, choosing which college to attend, or listening for what thought wants to be tweeted, sharpen your instincts.

7. Regularly ask yourself intuition-tapping questions. In no particular order, try these:

   • What do I need to remember to be most aware of right now?

   • What is my path right now?

   • What do I need to do to take care of myself right now?

   • What is it that I don't want to know about myself?

   • What am I not saying?

   • What message is my body trying to give me right now?

8. Remember: Off the top of your head usually means from the bottom of your heart. Beatnik author William Burroughs was right, "Rewrites are a betrayal of your own thoughts." Don't edit yourself. Words contain truths.

Chapter 5
CAREER

Please don't tell me I have to live with my parents forever!

~~~~~~

How many times have people asked you what you want to be when you grow up? When you're little, it's easy, right? You probably wanted to be a princess, an actress, a professional athlete, or a singer. It was simple back then, but then you figured out very few people get to be successful in those jobs, and you might have had to change your mind. You may have felt you needed to adopt more "realistic" career aspirations. If you already have a good idea about all of this—congratulations! You're way ahead of the game. If you're feeling clueless, welcome to the club! You're in the majority. Even if you already have an idea, it could still change. Life has a way of doing that to you. You don't have to know exactly what you want to do just yet. It just may be time to start thinking about which path you want to be on—college, vocational training, military, starving artist, etc.

As I mentioned in chapter 4, I went to college (Michigan State University—Go Spartans!) and enrolled as an accounting major as a freshman. I took a full year of classes (many of which were general education classes) and realized accounting was not a great fit for me. I needed more time interacting with others and feared the idea of crunching numbers for hours on end in a dimly lit cubicle all by myself. I did well enough to pass the classes, but I had no real passion for accounting. I'm not painting a very glamorous picture of accounting and completely realize that not all accounting jobs would be like this, but in my nightmare future—it was.

I explored my options and thought back to what I'd enjoyed in the past. Even as a kid, I was curious about how the brain worked and why people did the things they did. When I was eight, I told my mom that I wanted to be either a psychologist or a psychiatrist, but I couldn't decide which one. My mom helped me create a questionnaire that we printed and mailed to local psychologists and psychiatrists, asking about their education, job, and overall satisfaction. (Good mom, right?). This was well before the convenience of the Internet and email. To their credit, nearly everyone we sent it to filled the questionnaire out and mailed it back.

Now, here I was in college, an unhappy accounting major, wondering how I had deviated from my original plan. I realized it was fear. I was afraid to commit to a career that required roughly ten years of college. Mine measured out to four years for my bachelor's degree, two years for my master's degree, and four years for my doctorate degree. When I sat down and really thought it over, I decided (for me) I'd rather invest extra time (and money) on the front end to commit to a career I'd enjoy, rather than have a shorter educational investment and take the risk I might hate going to work every day. I switched my major and haven't looked back since. You'll need to figure out which formula works best for you.

There are a number of factors that need to be considered in your career choice. What type of training is required to do the job and are you willing to invest (time, energy, and money) in that training? Would you enjoy the daily activities related to your chosen field? You're not going to love your job every day— no one does, but you do want to enjoy it most of the time. How available are jobs in your chosen profession? If your dream job only has a few openings, you're possibly going to have tons of competition for those spots. I'm not telling you to change your direction, but it should be a factor in your decision. Go in with your eyes wide open.

Do what makes you happy and proud of yourself.

Aimee Teegarden—actress, model

Enjoying your career is so incredibly important. No one wants to wake up each day and feel like, "Ugh! Do I have to go in today?" It would be a sucky way to live your life. Find something that you enjoy more often than not—every day won't be a party, but it shouldn't be prison either. Unless you want to work in prisons—totally your choice! There's a saying, "Do what you love and you'll never work a day in your life." I love the idea, but it's somewhat misleading. There will be times when your job will be "work," but if you love it, it's definitely more tolerable during these times.

You also want to feel proud of your accomplishments and what you're contributing to the world. You may not be creating the cure for cancer, but it helps to feel that what you're doing matters. This will help you get through the days when your job is frustrating, your coworkers are irritating, and you have to get out of bed when you really want to sleep in. Try to avoid what others think should make you happy. Your career can't be about what they want for you. You'll likely work in some capacity for thirty plus years. That's way too long to be unhappy.

The best piece of advice that I received as a teen was very simple but significant enough to change my life forever. I was told to "pursue a career in something that you believe in and enjoy what you're doing."

At the time I had to really stop and consider what I was hearing since this concept went against the ideals under which I was raised. In my family, I was expected to be one of three things: a doctor, a lawyer or an engineer. Ultimately, it was this small piece of advice which compelled me to build my own path toward a career that was not expected of me, but that I found to be fulfilling and enjoyable. It did not take long for me to realize that my true passion was in public service.

As an immigrant, I find happiness in giving back to the country that provided my family and me with a new life and opportunities. The sense of joy and pride that this nation invokes in me led me to devote my life to public service. In this career, far from what my family envisioned for me, I have achieved many accomplishments that neither I, nor they, ever thought possible. Today, I am honored to be named the first Asian-American and the first Vietnamese-American to serve on the Orange County Board of Supervisors, the youngest Supervisor elected in Orange County history, as well as the highest ranking Vietnamese-American woman elected official in the United States.

I would never have achieved any of this had I not been advised to pursue a career that motivates and inspire me and, more importantly, that makes me happy while giving back to this great nation and helping others.

Supervisor Janet Nguyen—(Orange) County supervisor

This flows so well with Aimee Teagarden's quote. The simplest path to career satisfaction is finding something that makes you happy and provides a feeling of accomplishment. When I was little, my grandfather determined that I, out of all the grandchildren, should follow in his footsteps and become an engineer. I'm not sure how I was the chosen grandchild—

was I good at math? Did he tell us all the same thing? Or was I randomly selected as his mini me? I think it was because I was close to his youngest grandchild, and all of the others had already rejected the idea.

All very sweet, but, unfortunately for both of us, I never had the slightest inclination toward engineering. Engineering is a fantastic career and he'd raised a family as an engineer, and I imagine I may have been able to do so as well. Here's the problem. It's very unlikely that I could have been happy. Your career should ideally include some activities you would do even if you weren't being paid. Not that anyone should expect you to work for free; you have bills to pay, right?

Let's talk a bit about having choices in your life. Do you want to know the best way to give yourself more choices as far as your future career? Get an education—whether this is in college or some form of vocational program. Not doing so can be so incredibly limiting. All too often I hear people complain that they don't have money for school. I get it—an education is expensive, but there are a number of options available to you. You can attend a community or junior college for your first two years as an undergrad at considerable savings, and then you can transfer to a four-year college or university when you're ready. You can apply for scholarships or grants. Every year tons of available money goes unclaimed. Apply for them! You can also take out loans.

I understand not wanting to take on debt. It's scary to think that you will finish college with a substantial debt hanging over your head, but statistics show that a college graduate can earn between $800,000 and $1.2 million more than a high school graduate over the course of their career. I had to take out loans for graduate school and was disheartened to realize that what I owed in student loans added up to what a very nice house in Michigan would cost when I was done. At this point, I anticipate having my loans paid off just in time to send Charlie to college, but that's the breaks. It was an investment in me and, for me, it paid off. Maybe I could've cut corners a little bit and could've borrowed a bit less.

> You can be and do anything you want in life; there is only one obstacle ... YOURSELF! Believe you can do it and you will succeed!
>
> **Maria Bravo**—philanthropreneur

There are so many ways that we get in our own way and interfere with our ability to achieve success. You may stop focusing on yourself and your goals and instead may focus on relationships with other people (i.e., boyfriends, girlfriends, and especially other friends). You can spend so much time with them and thinking about them that your own work just doesn't get done. You can be so afraid of failure that you never try in the first place. Read the chapter on failure to see why it isn't something to fear—the only real regret is never really trying.

Do you notice a common theme here? You. You're the #1 thing that can get in your way. Remember when we talked about goals and how you'll have both long and short term goals? You career is planned out much the same way. Those things you can be working on now to prepare yourself for your career (i.e., going to school, maintaining a clean criminal record, and avoiding behaviors that could interfere with success, like drugs) are your short term goals and behaviors. There are also longer term goals or behaviors, like preparing for college or whatever vocational training your future career might require. You're the most important factor in your own future success.

I have a client who is going to college in her thirties after having skipped it in her twenties. She has a tendency to beat herself up over "wasting" ten to fifteen years by not going to school earlier. This tendency to beat herself up interferes with her current successes. She can get so focused on what she didn't do that she fails to take pride in what she's doing now. If you have changed past behaviors, let go of your guilt about them. Believe in yourself and be proud of the different choices you're making today.

If you can make something you love into a career, you will find great happiness.

Stacey Bendet Eisner—designer of Alice + Olivia

OK—reality check time. Not every job you will ever work will be your dream job. There will likely be many, many, many non-dream jobs first. Suck it up. It's called paying your dues. You may have to work to put yourself through college or whatever kind of training your dream job requires. You may have to work your way up through the field to get to your dream job. There are tons of reasons you may have to take on other jobs first as you pave your way. I worked in a shoe store. I was a waitress. I was a bartender. I was an extra on television and movie sets— basically a human prop.

The important thing is to keep your eyes on the prize. For me, these were all jobs that allowed me to support myself while I was working toward my bigger goal. I was putting food on the table and covering my rent while I was an undergraduate student in college and then later as a student in graduate school. As long as you're continuing to work toward your end goal, you're still on the path. No job is beneath you. If you don't like what you're doing, look for something else, but keep your eye on the prize.

If at all possible, never quit a job until you have another one to take its place. You need cash to survive and pay bills. There are definite exceptions to this rule—if your safety is ever at risk, get out. No job is ever worth sacrificing your life or overall well-being.

To teens: just because you have said "yes" doesn't mean you have to keep saying "yes." You are what you tweet to employers.

Elisabeth Hasselbeck—television personality, talk show host

There are a lot of levels to this quote. Let's start at the beginning. You always have the right to change your mind. This is in any situation, at any time. Just because you have agreed to something doesn't mean you're locked in (except maybe with the military). It's not just a lady's prerogative to change her mind—it's anyone's. If you get more information, or just have more time to think things through, and this causes you to question whether or not you're in—then you're free to be out.

There's always a way to get out of any choice you've made (maybe even the military), but you need to take a stand. You'll need to make your change of heart known through your words and your actions. You can't assume people can read your mind and know what you want. Tell them so there's no confusion. This applies to everything (sex is most definitely included). Don't ever feel because you have already said yes that you're locked in. Change your mind as often as needed for you to be comfortable with your decision.

Be careful what you put on the Internet. Don't ever post anything you wouldn't want your mother, grandmother, future children, and any future employer to see. Once something is posted, it can never really be deleted. Chances are they will have the opportunity to see anything you post whether you like it or not. Employers now google new applicants prior to even interviewing them (and definitely before they hire them). You may think it's fun to post pictures of yourself partying it up with friends or spouting off various profanity-laden opinions, but your future employers might not be so impressed.

Anything and everything you post on the Internet is there forever. You have no way of making it go away. Be careful about what you post. Please use extreme caution about what your friends post about you. It will follow you forever. (I'll say once again how relieved I am that neither the Internet nor cell phones were common while I was in college. I could NEVER run for president if there was photographic proof of some of the things I did. I promise, I am not running for president anyway—just in case.)

How to figure out what to do to support yourself:

1. **Make a list of all the things you like to do**. Make a second list of all the things you do well. Don't censor these lists. List everything you can possibly think of. Start to think about careers that might allow you to do those things you're both good at and enjoy. OK—you like to play video games, which are unlikely to become a paying gig, but there are definite careers in video game design and production. Think outside the box!

2. **Think about where you would like to work**. I'm not talking about a specific place, but do you want to be indoors or outdoors? Do you prefer a regular 9to5 schedule or more flexibility? Do you want to work in a quiet space (like a cubicle), or do you need more stimulation? Are you a social beast, or do you prefer working alone? Does the idea of interacting with customers fill you with excitement or dread? Does the idea of structure make you feel safe or trapped? Make a list of your responses if this will help you organize your thoughts. Sometimes writing things down can help you find clarity.

3. **Think about where you stand on work-life balance**. How much of your life do you want to dedicate to your career, and how important is it to move up in the company? Do you thrive under pressure or tear your hair out? Are you OK with a job that might come home with you at the end of the day, or are you looking for one that you can leave at the office? Are you looking

to make big bucks, or are you happy to pay the bills? What role might a family play in your future plans?

4. **Take a career assessment test to help sort out fields that might fit your personality and interests**. These can often be found online, in career advice books, and in school counseling centers. Consider your test results. Get rid of anything that doesn't fit. I was once assessed to be a future florist. I wanted to work in an office with a set schedule, so I was able to cross this off of my list. These results are most useful at pointing you in a general direction.

5. **Find people in your possible career choices and have an honest conversation with them**. Many people are open to discussing what they like and dislike about their careers. Remember the questionnaire I created when I was eight years old? Tread lightly on sensitive topics, such as how much money they make. This is private information most won't want to share, and some may be offended by such questions. Maybe you can intern to get a firsthand experience of what the job may be like on a daily basis.

6. **Start doing research to determine what you may need to do to earn your chosen career**. Do you need college or vocational training? Does the industry offer on-the-job training? Are there certain jobs that would provide the experience necessary for your chosen career? Maintain your path until you can get there!

7. **If picking your career feels like way too much pressure right now—take a breath and relax**. Sometimes you

need time to grow and develop before things become clearer. Sometimes your plan even changes—remember I started out as an accounting major! Just don't drop it completely. Do what feels best for today and keep evaluating the future.

Chapter 6

FINANCES

*What to do with all of
your fabulous loot and how
to avoid going broke*

~~~~~~~~~~~~~~~~~~~~~~~~~~~~~

My lovelies, my lovelies, you need to be careful with your money. Debt can be a scary, scary thing. As soon as you turn eighteen, you'll be inundated with credit card applications and offers for financing. They'll offer you all kinds of things in order to get you to apply for their credit card. Many stores have their own credit card and will offer you a discount for applying for the card—even if you aren't approved. All of this sounds enchanting, right? Who doesn't want 15 percent off the clothes they're buying anyway? The slippery slope comes in having to pay it back later. All too often credit card shopping doesn't feel like you're spending real money. Then the bill comes. Cue the creepy music. They'll no longer be your good friends when you're unable to pay your bills. The mean debt collection phone calls will begin, and they're super aggressive.

When I went to college, there were booths from various credit card companies set up all over Welcome Week offering great goodies (i.e., T-shirts, water bottles, food, gift cards) in exchange for completing credit card applications. They knew we were college students with little to no money, but we were immediately approved anyway. They were banking on our future college graduate income as well as our ability to run to our parents if finances became too hairy. The goodies were definitely not worth the pounding our credit could (and for many did) take if we would be unable to pay.

In college, I had two roommates who found themselves buried in credit card debt. This was in the days before cell phones, so we all shared one landline. These lovely ladies never answered the phone—I mean NEVER. The rest of us would answer the phone whenever it rang and would tell the collection agent they weren't home. If you haven't seen the movie *Confessions of a Shopaholic* starring Isla Fisher, you should google it. In it, Isla plays a young woman living beyond her means via credit cards and her many attempts to avoid the collection agent on her tail. You don't want to become this woman. Do your best to live within your means at all times—only spend what you have and, ideally, not all of it.

Work so you appreciate the value of money.

Becky Quick—television journalist/newscaster,

co-anchorwoman of CNBC's

Financial News Show Squawk Box

There's no better way to realize the value of money than to earn it yourself. When you're pulling in $10/hour, all of a sudden those new shoes you have to have can seem awfully expensive. You can actually calculate how many hours you'd need to work to pay for something yourself and fully appreciate the cost—it may even help you appreciate it more when someone (like your parents) pay for it on your behalf.

My first job was at shoe store. A really crappy shoe store that I won't name in case they're still in business and might sue me for saying they're crappy. I was fifteen or sixteen and was looking for anyone who would pay me enough money to put gas in my car and have a little left over for spending money. I was absolutely floored by how much of my check was taken out for taxes each week. I was already being paid a pittance each hour (back in the "olden days" minimum wage was much lower than it is now.) I worked there for roughly six months before my new part in the school play necessitated that I quit. I was devastated (not really). But I was a little more grateful for the money my mom was willing to kick my way since I was now unemployed. Probably not grateful enough—thanks, Mom.

Save something out of every dollar you earn, &
don't ever carry credit card debt.

Liz Pulliam Weston—personal
finance columnist, author

Saving money is really hard. There's always something
you want or need, and typically you aren't making very much
money. Despite the challenge, it's definitely a good idea to have
a nest egg to fall back on in case of an unexpected expense.
Unexpected expenses can be fun or not so fun. If you have a car,
you might get a flat tire or dead battery. It could be something
exciting like concert tickets to see your favorite band. You might
lose your job and need some money to get by until you can
land the next job. Whatever the reason, you'll appreciate having
some money socked away for such a situation.

The important thing to remember is you need to replenish
the savings as soon as possible after you use it. Decide how
much of each paycheck you can stash away and stick to it.
Make it one of your regular bills each month. As you're paying
your credit card or cell phone bill each month, put that $20
(or however much you've chosen) into your savings as well—
consider it paying yourself.

Credit cards are dangerous, my friends. I know I already
told you about the pains in the butt that collection agents are,
but now let's talk about interest rates and minimum payments.
Your goals should be to pay off any credit card each and every
month. Why? You'll pay through the nose in interest otherwise.
Let me give you an example: Let's say you're given a store credit
card for your favorite clothing store. They usually will start you

out with a $500.00 limit. Store credit cards are notorious for having higher interest rates than Visa or MasterCard, so let's assume you end up with a 20percent interest rate.

Most of us are super excited when we get our first credit card and go on a shopping spree. Before you know it, you've maxed out your card and owe $500. Not the end of the world, right? Especially since your card is so understanding and only requires a $15 per month minimum payment. How considerate of them! You can manage $15—score!

Here's the downside—even if you never spend another dime on the credit card, you'll be paying for those clothes for fifty months. Seriously, it will take you four years and two months to pay off the $500 balance if you pay $15 each month, AND you'll have paid an additional $236 in interest. You'll have paid $736 for $500 in clothes that you probably haven't worn in several years. Does that sound like a good deal anymore?

There was a point when I was in graduate school and my husband was a fairly new college graduate that we racked up some healthy (or unhealthy) credit card debt. It was ugly. We owed more than I made a year as a graduate assistant, and we were stretched fairly tight financially. We had what we refer to as a "come to Jesus" moment. We had to sit down and seriously look at our finances. We had to consolidate all of our credit cards (and there were many) and put them on a card with the lowest interest rate we could get. Then we started the process of hammering away at the debt until it was paid off. It took YEARS.

Don't put yourself in this position if you can avoid it. Live within your means. Even better, live below your means and sack the extra away into your savings as personal finance expert Cait Flanders suggests. The "things" you buy that you'll undoubtedly be sick of in a few months are definitely not worth the unnecessary stress debt can cause.

> Saving sounds boring but it's essential to live the life they'll one day want and buying "things" won't make them happy.
>
> **Cait Flanders**—personal finance blogger

Saving is super important. You may be saving for a car, a vacation, the down payment for a house, or your retirement. All of these require saving as most of us will never have enough money readily available for these things. Decide what your savings plan is going to be—whether it's a certain amount each week or a percentage of each check. Next, pay yourself just like you would pay any other bill. All too often we fail to pay into our savings when money gets tight. Consider it a necessity like your rent or cell phone bill. I even have it set up that my bank account automatically transfers a specific amount on the fifteenth of each month directly from my checking account to my savings account.

I'm a fan of retail therapy—you know, shopping to make yourself feel better. There's a big but here... you can shop yourself into worse trouble. "Things" can't make you happy, and shopping yourself into debt will only make the situation harder for you. If you're unhappy, find something to make you feel better—chances are, though, it isn't for sale at the mall. I already referred to being super broke in graduate school.

My husband wasn't making a ton of money, and I was making next to nothing as a graduate assistant. We would often have to choose between going to the grocery store and seeing a movie. Finding inexpensive ways to have fun became not only a goal but a necessity. There are tons of things you can do—go for a hike, visit a museum on a free night, or see a movie at the cheap theater. (We still call it the dollar theater, but I know it's usually $2 these days). Bottom line: find ways to feel better without breaking the bank. You don't want to add "further in debt" to your list of problems.

Don't be afraid to talk about money. When offered pay, ask for more. Men and boys do it naturally. So should girls.

Helaine Olen—journalist, author, blogger

There's still a double standard in the way we expect men and women to deal with money and financial matters. Honestly, there's a double standard in how we expect men and women to behave in a number of situations. Let's focus on money for now. All too often there's an expectation that men will be aggressive/assertive and women will be quiet and "grateful." Crapola. You don't have to be a jerk, but you should stand up for yourself. Know your value and expect others to recognize and treat you with that value. If not, help them understand just how much you're worth. You don't have to accept the first offer from anyone. There's always room to consider negotiation. This applies to your salary, buying or selling a car, or anywhere else money is involved.

A willingness and readiness to be open to talking about money should be present in relationships as well. You'll want to make sure you and your partner are open with one another about money—both in regards to the spending and saving of it. All too often I have seen relationships go sideways when the primary area of conflict is financial. Get on the same page ahead of time, and it can save you tons of drama later. You should talk about what you want to spend money on—what your priorities are for purchases—and how aggressively you want to save it and for what (i.e., retirement, home, vacations). You should talk about whether to have shared or separate bank accounts. How are you going to divide the bills? Having these conversations openly can help reduce potential conflicts in the future.

When I was in graduate school, my husband covered 90percent of our bills each month. This placed a lot of pressure on him. He had to stay at a job he didn't love where he worked long hours so he could support us. Once I finished school and began to bring in my own income, he was able to quit that position and take one for less money, but a better work/life balance. We had negotiated this dynamic well ahead of time. If we hadn't, there was potential for significant resentment on his part. Talk through these situations to avoid hurt feelings and conflict later.

Be Thankful: As a teen, even though you feel overworked and annoyed by everyone telling you what to do all the time, you are in a unique time of your life when everything you have is given to you. Your parents, community, mentors and/

or school scholarships make it possible for you to get an education, sleep with a roof over your head and have regular meals without working for it. Once you become an "adult," you will be expected to provide these things for yourself. So, be grateful and express your thanks to your parents, mentors, teachers and anyone else who is giving, so that you can get the education you need to build a solid foundation for your life.

Natalie Pace—author, CEO, philanthropist, and founder of Women's Investment Network, LLC

I wholeheartedly admit being a teenager is hard. It's really, really hard. At the same time, you have so much to be thankful for. As you get older, life gets harder in different ways. You'll look back on these years and regret not fully appreciating all the help that was available to you. Whether it's the place to live that your parents provided or your mom doing your laundry. It could be the extra help provided by a teacher when you were confused or frustrated. These are all things that are currently available to you free of charge. Appreciate it while you can. If I want someone to do my laundry, I have to pay them (or beg my husband).

All of these things can be ridiculously expensive. Everything you're getting for free these days will one day cost you a ton of money. You'll have to pay someone to clean your house, provide tutoring, and prepare meals, or do it yourself. You'll have to buy your own groceries, clothing, and school supplies. If any of this is currently being provided by your parents, appreciate it. Let them know that you appreciate it—not just when they upgrade your cell phone.

It's funny. Every so often a group of my friends will get together to hang out. Conversation sometimes turns to nostalgia for our teen years. It isn't the friends and exes that we necessarily miss, but we miss having other people do things for us. It's the freedom from having to be a grown-up and making all kinds of decisions. I think our memory of this time in our lives tends to be a bit biased. I don't think anyone really wants to give up the control we have over our lives and become a teenager again, but the fantasy can be appealing.

This probably happens across all ages of our lives. My daughter fantasizes about being a grown-up ("It will be so easy!"), my friends fantasize about being kids again ("It was so easy!"), and many teens fantasize about being in their twenties ("It will be so easy!"). There's this idea out there that everyone else has it better or easier. Remember, there are pros and cons to every age you'll ever be. Not only will you gain some desirable freedom and power as you age, but you'll also gain responsibility and stress. Remember the line from *Spiderman*, "With great power, comes great responsibility."

How to manage your cashola:

1. **Do your research on credit cards**. There are a number of websites that allow you to calculate how long it will take you to pay off specific amounts based on various interest rates. You can play with it—it's very user friendly—and you'll be amazed at how expensive credit can actually be. One of the websites is: http://

www.bankrate.com/calculators/credit-cards/credit-card-payoff-calculator.aspx/. You can also get more information about credit cards in general, as well as many of the terms used by credit card companies, at http://www.studentcredit.com/learn.htm/.

2. **You need to have money to start managing it, so you need to start thinking about where the money is going to come from**. Are you going to get a job? Do you have family who gifts money for birthdays and holidays? Do your parents give you an allowance for expenses each month?

3. **Be wary of borrowing money**. Over the course of your life, there will be tons of things you'll want to buy and not enough money on hand to get them. You'll be tempted to borrow money to get them. You may hit up your parents, but this doesn't put you in a good position for the future. Your best bet is to learn early on how to live within your means. What does this mean? It means only spend money you have and, ideally, not all of it. If you start using a credit card, only charge what you can pay off in full each month.

4. **Learn how to live according to a budget**. I must be honest here. I was not good at this until my mid to late twenties. (OK, maybe it was my thirties.) I want it to be easier for you. Start thinking about how much money you have available each month. Look at your bills for that month. Do you have enough to cover them? If the answer is "no," then you have two choices—either find a way to earn more money or start cutting back on your

bills. I was shocked when I looked at how much I was spending at Starbucks each month—and I don't even drink coffee! Part of your budget can also be saving money toward a big purchase. Say you want to go on a trip with friends after graduation and it's going to cost you $500. You may start putting $50 away each month beginning in July, so you'll have the funds available to you in May of the next year.

5. **Start learning now the difference between your wants and your needs**. There are limitless things that you might want in this world, but there are few things that you actually need. When you find yourself out shopping and are ready to make a purchase, take a moment to ask the question, "Do I really need this, or do I want it?" If you need it, figure out a way to pay for the item. If you only want it, then ask yourself if you have extra money available right now. If not, don't stretch your finances unnecessarily.

6. **You live in a world where everything is online**. You need to protect your financial identity online.

   • Never respond to an email from your bank asking for your details. Your bank will never email you asking for any personal or account details—after all, they have all these details, don't they? No, this is a scam and as soon as you send your account details, date of birth, credit card number, or even just the expiration date of your cards, you're at risk of your accounts being used fraudulently.

- Look for a secure URL. Before you enter your account details into any site, whether it be online banking or an online store, look at the address bar and make sure it reads https:// as the 's' means the site is secure, and your details will be protected.

- Protect your paperwork. Don't write down your PIN or credit card number and especially don't keep your card and PIN together—even the bank will mail them to you in two separate envelopes. Also make sure that if you're throwing away receipts or statements, shred them to avoid leaving your personal details in the trash for anyone to find.

7. **Consider the cost of items to make the best choice for you and your current circumstances**. When we all started buying new cars as adults, I noticed my friends buying more and more expensive cars. Consider your purchases—just because you can afford it, doesn't mean you should be spending the money. When you start comparing colleges and deciding where to go, consider how much they're going to cost you. What kind of return can you expect on your investment? Is the cost of the private college worth the additional benefits?

8. **Health insurance is important**. Stay on your parents' insurance as long as you're legally able and get your own as soon as you're removed from their insurance. An illness or accident doesn't have to be catastrophic to be incredibly expensive, and you don't need to take on that type of debt if you can avoid it.

9. **Have a nest egg**. The general rule of thumb is that you should have savings that would cover three months' worth of your bills. If you don't have it now, start putting it away until you get there. You'll be relieved to have this cushion if you should lose your job unexpectedly and need time to find a new one.

10. **Pay your bills on time**! I'm going to throw my husband under the bus here. When we met, in college, we were both working in a bar/restaurant where we made good money, especially when you considered how low our bills were. We made enough to cover our expenses with some left over for fun. My husband's philosophy was that his creditors shouldn't care *when* they got paid as long as they did. He would sit down and pay all of his bills every few months. Well…everything was late and his creditors *did* care. His credit score took a hit unnecessarily. Your credit score helps determine whether or not a bank will loan you money and what type of rate you'll receive on the money. This applies to future car loans, credit cards, and mortgages. The easiest thing you can do to boost your credit score is to pay your bills on time, every time.

Chapter 7

FAILURE AND REJECTION

Ouch, that hurts! Now what?

~~~~~~~~~~~~~~~~~~~~~~~~~~~~~~

Do not be afraid to take a risk. It is great to be successful, rest on our laurels, and always make safe choices, but in the end we learn more from those moments when we fall short and fail. Allowing our mistakes to help us grow expands our horizons and moves us to create a brighter future for ourselves and for others. The world moves forward every day because someone is willing to take the risk. You can be that someone.

Rabbi Sally J. Priesand—America's first female rabbi ordained by a rabbinical seminary

Smart. Some of the most successful people in the world initially failed, but what makes them stand out now is they didn't give up. Bill Gates (founder of Microsoft) failed at his first businesses. The famous secret chicken recipe of Harland David Sanders (better known as Colonel Sanders of Kentucky Fried Chicken fame) was rejected 1009 times before being accepted by a restaurant. Walt Disney was fired from his job at a newspaper because "he lacked imagination and had no good ideas." He then started a number of businesses that failed and he went into bankruptcy. Thomas Edison had over a 1000 failed attempts to invent the light bulb before finding one that would work.

Oprah Winfrey was once fired and deemed "unfit for TV." Marilyn Monroe had a tough childhood and was told by modeling agents she should become a secretary. Steven Spielberg was rejected by the University of Southern California School of Theater, Film and Television—three times. JK Rowling's books were initially rejected by twelve different publishers. Elvis Presley was fired by the manager of the Grand Ole Opry and told "You ain't goin' nowhere, son. You ought to go back to drivin' a truck." Michael Jordan was cut from his high school basketball team.

What did these people all have? Determination. They had a willingness to learn from their failures and keep pushing forward anyway. Sometimes they made modifications as a result of feedback (like Thomas Edison) and achieved success only because of what they learned in those failures. In fact, Thomas Edison often disputed the idea that he had failed at inventing the light bulb, but, instead, claimed he had discovered 1000 ways *not* to make a light bulb. Others refused to surrender to rejection and kept pushing forward until they found someone who appreciated their efforts (like Elvis Presley and Marilyn Monroe).

What type of person are you going to be? Was your failure because you need to try something else (i.e., improve your skills) or their bad judgment? If it's you that needs to improve, get to it. Take classes. Practice. Improve your skills to improve your chances. If their judgment is off, keep looking until you find someone who can recognize the value of what you have to offer. Either way—don't give up. Your job is not yet done. Get to work.

Failure. There are few things that most people dread more than failure. You try something and it doesn't work out the way you want and hope. Oftentimes you're embarrassed and don't want other people to know about it. You likely feel like crap and wish you had never put yourself out there in the first place. Shake it off, my friend. It's time to pull on your big girl pants. The great tragedy isn't failing, but that the fear of failure often terrifies us into inaction. We never try at all.

Failure isn't the worst thing that can happen to you. Not trying is so much worse. You can miss out on life's opportunities, and all that you can learn through your experiences, if you're too afraid to take a risk. Try out for the school musical or the soccer team. Apply for the job. Study hard for the test. Apply to a "reach school" for college. Talk to a cute boy (or girl). If it turns out the way you hope—fabulous, but if it doesn't, be proud of yourself for your bravery and learn from the experience. What can/should you do differently next time in hopes of getting your desired outcome? Learn from your "failures" and see them as opportunities, not as roadblocks.

Not only is failure not the end of the world, but it may be the next step in the most amazing journey of your life. There are so many opportunities that can grow out of your disappointments. Find the opportunities in these failures. I applied to a number of colleges over the years—some for undergrad and some for grad school. I didn't get into them all—I know, shocking, right? Who wouldn't want me? I can pinpoint so many things in my life I would've lost had I gotten into the schools that rejected me. If I wouldn't have gone to Michigan State University for my undergrad, I probably wouldn't have met my husband. I also wouldn't have met some of the best friends a girl can have. If I hadn't come out to Pepperdine for graduate school, I likely wouldn't be living in beautiful Southern California. I wouldn't have had opportunities like working at CHLA. I only have these things because I failed to get into other schools (even though I may not have chosen them anyway). Remember to look for the good opportunities that come out of failures or rejections.

I also think it's very important to realize that we all make mistakes, have issues, insecurities and so forth. Many seem to think they're alone or have the worst of problems, but trust me you're not alone; we all have our underlying issues. The same way people in public places wouldn't know some of your issues, you don't know theirs. Just remember nobody's perfect. It's those mistakes and challenges that shape us into the people we are. Every challenge makes us stronger, and if you're going through something difficult, know that it ALWAYS gets better. No matter how impossible that seems, know in your heart that you will become ten times stronger from that challenge. I promise.

Always remember to live your life to the fullest and never look back in regret, it's pointless. We can only learn and grow from our mistakes. It's never too late to turn your life around of make a difference. Greatness has been achieved at all ages. You never know whose life you're meant to change.

Cassie Scerbo—American singer, actress, dancer

It can often feel as though there's a giant spotlight on your failures. It seems all the world is watching and laughing as we fall on our face. This isn't usually the case. We're, often, self-involved creatures. We're so busy focusing on ourselves that we have little time to focus on everyone else. I think this is why our failures always seem so large to us. We're focused on it to such an extent that we can't be rational in considering others' failures. You're far from the first to fail, and you won't be the last. I can personally guarantee it. Give yourself a brief moment to lick your wounds and move on.

There are always going to be those people who seem to celebrate your mistakes and enjoy it when you trip and fall. You know the type. They're either directly or indirectly rude. The direct brat might say something like, "You didn't really think you were going to be cast in the play, did you? Seriously!" The indirect brat is a wee bit more of a trickster. You may be tempted to take her at face value until you understand the meanness behind her kind words. She may come up and say, "I'm so bummed you didn't get the part. I had my fingers crossed for you." Sounds sweet, right? The problem is her smile may not quite reach her eyes, her tone may not match the sincerity of her words, and there are likely whispers in the hall of not-so-nice things she has said about you. How should you handle these "ladies"? Forget them. Remember we talked about self-esteem in chapter 2? People who feel good about themselves don't need to tear others down. If one of these princesses approaches you like her bratty self, then just smile, walk away and invest your time in people who genuinely care about you.

Too often, once something doesn't work out the way we had hoped, we give up. I tried learning to swim as a kid and wasn't good at it right away. (I was actually terrible—had to be pulled out by lifeguards and everything.) So I stopped trying. I won't drown in a pool (barring some tragic accident), but you throw me in the ocean and I'm a goner. At this point, I'll need my eight-year-old daughter to pull me to safety. (She's a great swimmer.)

If I could go back and talk to my younger self, I'd tell her to, "Suck it up!" Few things in life come easily or naturally. Sometimes you need to flounder around (a *Little Mermaid* pun) before you can figure things out and get better. Practice would've made a world of difference. I guess this is something I could still work on. Maybe I need to call the local pool and set up some lessons. If only I could guarantee that no one would watch—my husband says I look comical…Let's just say there are no Olympic hopes in my future.

Let go of your fears.

Jessika Van—actress, singer-songwriter, pianist, dancer

Don't let fear stop you from doing all you want to do with your life. In those moments when you feel like you're being overwhelmed by fear, take a long, slow, deep breath. Maybe take another. Ask yourself what is the worst that can happen. Typically, the response is not death or dismemberment. (If it is—stop and reconsider. Death is not to be played with…). Usually the fear is being embarrassed or disappointed. You can survive both of these. There might be some marginal amounts of emotional pain, but you can and will survive. Use the fear to motivate you and make yourself stronger.

An important lesson that I didn't learn until adulthood is that you can manage other people's reactions to your failure. For instance, say you're applying to a college and you have little chance of being accepted. If you talk about it all of the time and are unrealistic ("cocky") about your chance of getting in, then people will be tempted to mock you ruthlessly if you're not accepted. You're setting yourself up for the easy smack down. People like to see arrogant people fall on their face. Pride goeth before the fall or something like that.

If you acknowledge it's a reach and you're simply trying to see what happens and don't get in, you'll find people are more supportive and understanding. If you act like it's the end of the world, others will react differently too. Generally people will only make as big a deal as you do. For instance, if you're walking along and trip over your own feet, you can a) run out of the room crying or b) jump up and say, "ta-daa." Which situation will likely blow over faster? Sometimes people will only make a big deal out of your missteps if you do so first. Take that long, slow, deep breath and think before you react.

Courage is feeling fear and doing it anyway. Do the things that scare you.

Stacy London—stylist/fashion consultant, author, television co-host

---

It's easy to try things that don't scare you. There's not much bravery in any of that. True courage is in facing the things that scare the crap out of you and giving them a try anyway. In all honesty, it may not go well, but you'll have the satisfaction of having tried. Someone (I don't really remember who) once told me that the biggest failure is the regret that comes from not going for it. Don't live your life full of regrets or "what might have been." Learn how to try your best and shake off the hurt feelings if you fall short.

I was raised to be terrified of roller coasters. My fear of these rides was cultivated throughout my childhood by my mother who couldn't tolerate any rides that went fast, twisted, turned, or, heaven forbid, went upside down. I was convinced I wouldn't survive such an experience and dutifully avoided them like the plague. I was afraid I would throw up, cry, or something else equally embarrassing. I would fail.

At amusement parks, I would stand in line with friends and use the "chicken door" when we got to the front. (For those who don't know—the chicken door is the escape exit for those who change their minds about a ride. I hadn't changed my mind, but I'd never planned to try in the first place.) I did this for years. It was a major failure in my book. Then my daughter was born and was naturally a daredevil. She wanted to ride EVERYTHING! I had this picture in my head of sitting around at Disneyland bored out of my mind while she and her dad went on rides having a great time.

Even worse, I worried that my daughter would learn from me that rides were not safe and lose her fearless attitude. I didn't want to make her afraid. So, instead, I made a plan. I needed to change my strategies. I talked myself off the ledge and thought about the worst thing that could happen. OK—I could throw up. Gross, but survivable. I could start crying. Embarrassing, but how many people at Disneyland would I ever see again? I realized there were very few worst case scenarios that I couldn't survive. I started out small and worked my way up to the bigger rides—granted Disneyland doesn't have anything too terrifying. Before I knew it, I was my daughter's plus-one on the rides—though sometimes she still likes to ride with her daddy.

Look upon the most embarrassing moments as fantastic future anecdotes.

Alexa Chung—television presenter, model, and contributing editor at British *Vogue*

I love this! Learning to laugh at yourself is one of the most important lessons you can ever learn. If everything in life came easily for you, you'd be an incredible bore (and you'd only make everyone else feel bad about themselves.) Stories about your many successes come across as bragging, but there can be great humor and entertainment in why things went badly. Think of this misstep as material for your biography someday.

I have tons of these types of stories. For instance, there's the time I was fired as a graduate assistant while in my doctoral program at Pepperdine University. I was the assistant to the assistant (there may have been one more…to the assistant here) to the head of alumni relations for my department (Graduate School of Education and Psychology). I was terrible at it. I can admit that now. It was only made worse by the fact that I didn't care that I was terrible at it and it showed. One day my immediate boss was finally fed up with my incompetence and lack of desire to improve and unceremoniously dumped my butt. At first, it stung. I had a master's degree and was fired from a job that required me to update databases all day.

Seriously, I was updating databases about where alumni were working, whether they were married or had kids, etc. I was a little pissed—who the hell did she think she was? Oh yeah, she was my boss and I was a miserable employee. I can now make fun of just how terrible I was at this job—there are countless examples of my ineptitude. I shook it off and began looking for something that was a better fit for me. I realized I would try harder and care more about jobs that mattered more to me. Though I do have to admit, I still am a little hesitant when my Alumni Relations Department sends out donation requests. I can't help thinking, "Hey, you jerks fired me!" (Plus I'm still paying off my student loans—only ten more years!)

OK—your worst case scenario has happened. How do you manage failure?

1. **First and foremost, this is not the end of the world**. The zombie apocalypse has not befallen us. Someday you'll look back on this experience and it won't be painful. Take a deep breath and accept this as fact. It will get better. The sting will lessen.

2. **Allow yourself to feel the pain of your failure**. Don't ignore it. Let the anger, frustration, sadness, and hopelessness come to the surface so you can get rid of them and move on. Give yourself the opportunity to have a good wallow. It's important to remember that your wallow can't and shouldn't last forever. This is a short term pity party. At some point you'll need to acknowledge it sucks and move on.

3. **Try to find ways to take care of yourself**. Spend some time with friends or family. Don't try to hide in drugs or alcohol. It only makes the situation worse, and you'll end up feeling like a pile of crud. Don't spend time beating a dead horse about your failure; instead, distract yourself for a while. Have some fun. If you're into physical activities, go for a run. If you're a movie buff, check some out at your local theater. Give yourself a mini vacation from the failure for a while.

4. **Let go of perfectionism**. Changing your attitude about what failure means starts with accepting that few

things in this world can turn out exactly right the first time. Remember the examples of those now famous/successful people from the beginning of the chapter? Facing this reality lets you see the advantages of failure.

5. **Differentiate between what you did and who you are**. Failure is about doing things wrong. You can never BE a failure. You may have failed, but that's not who you are as a person. You still rock.

6. **Once you've had some time to deal with your feelings about failing, start thinking about what went wrong and why**. It's time to start thinking about what you might do differently next time. What were the things you had and didn't have? What did you do and didn't do? What were the things that you could control and couldn't control (*a college liking someone's admission essay better than yours is subjective and out of your control*)? Don't obsess and over analyze, but do give it some consideration—this will help you figure out what the heck to do next.

7. **Treat this failure as feedback**. Learn from what went wrong and make changes accordingly.

8. **Ask for help**. Connect with people who can give you advice and support. Maybe they can give you an outsider's perspective on what you can do differently next time.

9. **Try to keep perspective**. This is a huge deal to you (and it should be), but sometimes it can help to remember that there are others who have it much worse—starving children and the critically ill for example.

10. **Don't give up**! If this is something you really want, it's time to make a plan. Do you need to change your strategy? Take classes? Try harder?

11. **Finally, forgive yourself.** Don't beat yourself us just because it didn't work out. Give yourself credit for giving it your best effort.

Chapter 8

FINDING YOUR MORAL COMPASS

*You have to believe in something
(but you get to pick)*

~~~~~~~~~~~~~~~~~~~~~~

I originally intended to write this chapter about spirituality, specifically in relation to the world's various religions, but quickly realized that to many people, spirituality exists outside of popular religion. You can easily be spiritual without being remotely religious. It's not necessarily important that you subscribe to a specific religion or to its doctrine. The take away message from this chapter is you've got to believe in something. This is something that helps give your world order and allows you to explain how things happen and why. So instead, this chapter is about finding your moral compass—

the system you use to help you make decisions about how you'll be in the world.

Many identify three different forms of spirituality. The first is faith based—it's basically a belief in the ideals and rituals circulated by the various religious leaders or books. People depend entirely on their religious faith and follow the preaching and customs of the religious community. Often this is being Christian, Jewish, Muslim, Buddhist, etc. The second form of spirituality is knowledge based—using scientific or analytic processes to understand spirituality. Knowledge-based spirituality is about the understanding of things and the individual's desire to achieve knowledge about life based on her own goals and vision. This is typically accomplished through the use of modern science and experimentation to understand the world.

The final form of spirituality is mysticism based—seeking greater understanding by experiencing something beyond traditional reality often through such practices as meditation or prayer. These are usually independent practices that allow individual relationships with a higher power. Often people of a spiritual community may share a common spiritual theme— the path, work, practice, or tradition of identifying and taking in one's "true" nature and relationship to the rest of existence (God, creation (the universe), or life), and of becoming free of the lesser selfish persona in favor of being more fully one's "true" self.

People can seek their path to spirituality in a number of different ways. Some may seek purpose through traditional religious pursuits, such as Christianity, Judaism, or Islam (and many others). Others may explore meaning in their lives through the lens of environmentalism, science, or evolution. People also organize their world through sports, music, or art. It doesn't matter specifically how you find and define meaning in your life.

It matters that you have a framework within that you can use to explain the world around you in a way that makes sense to you. When life goes sideways on you, it can help to have a way to understand it, whether that be through Chaos Theory (very roughly that small changes in one system can lead to big changes in another) or Allah. The foundation of a belief system can provide feelings of safety and security.

> Create a strong relationship with God. People are human and sometimes they'll let you down, but keep your eyes on God and your purpose.
>
> **Jeannette Jenkins**—founder and president
> of the Hollywood Trainer Fitness Company,
> television host, author

This is applicable no matter how you define your spirituality and however you're seeking purpose and understanding in your life. As we discussed in chapter 2, people can definitely let you down at times—some on purpose and others unintentionally, but the result is still the same. You may feel angry, hurt, and generally disappointed in the behaviors of others, but where can you go with those feelings? Turn it over to your "higher power"—whatever that means to you. You may be able to find meaning behind the actions of others via your spirituality (i.e., God is testing you or human nature).

You can channel your frustrations and disappointments through your spiritual outlet. For instance, if you find your Zen on the soccer field, then you can head down to the field when upset and kick the ball around. Take some shots on goal. Refocusing your energy in a more positive direction can help you process through the upset and come out feeling better on the other side. Burn off all of that negative energy. This may be accomplished through dancing, painting, singing, or praying—whatever works for you. I'm an "over thinker" by nature—no real surprise there I suppose. So what do I do when things start going squirrely for me? I do best when I can take a run—somehow getting a chance to get out of my head and feel my body working calms me down. Find your thing and use it to center you.

Embrace life!

Allana Pratt—intimacy expert, television contributor and host

---

You only get one chance at your life. Live it with gusto! Celebrate all of your accomplishments and put energy toward those things that matter most to you. You can draw energy from your spiritual side to fuel this wonderful life you're living. Unfortunately, it won't always be rosy for you. There are a ridiculous number of challenges and disappointments that you may face while living your amazing life. There is really no way to avoid them all, no matter how hard you might try, and it wouldn't be in your best interest to avoid them all anyway. If you can, find a way to celebrate your challenges as well as your successes. These challenges are what help you grow. Here's another one of those sayings—what doesn't kill you makes you stronger. Focusing on what you're gaining from these challenges may take some of the sting out of them.

When my husband and I were dating in college, I was accepted into Pepperdine for graduate school while he still had a year to finish at Michigan State. This meant that we were going to have to be over 2000 miles apart for the better part of a year. This sucked. I wasn't happy about the separation. Most of our friends were commiserating with us about how awful the year was going to be, and our families were supportive but not always optimistic. None of this helped.

The best advice I received, strangely, was from a frequently drunk patron at the bar where we worked. He told me that this was likely to be one of the biggest challenges in our relationship, but if we could make it through the year, we could find comfort in the knowledge that this relationship has staying power. He said that we had to have faith that we could make it work. I found comfort in seeing this challenge as a testament to our relationship. It took some of the sting out of the separation and enabled me to be a bit more positive.

Stay true to your values and principles!
Karina Smirnoff—professional ballroom dancer
and television personality

All too often this is easier said than done. You'll face many situations in life where it would be easier for you to abandon your values and principles than to stand up for them. Remember, my brilliant ones, you are the one who will have to live with your choices and the consequences of those choices. Try not to sacrifice any part of yourself that you can't live without. There are so many situations where this could come into play. For instance, if you were to witness a group of girls ganging up on another girl (physically or emotionally) and you don't say anything—this may (I hope) conflict with your morals and values.

Do your best to act in accordance with your belief system. This is part of establishing your moral compass. What behaviors are you willing to tolerate and which will you oppose? Your moral compass may come from your religious beliefs (i.e., the Ten Commandments) or strategies associated with principles of fairness (i.e., good sportsmanship).

Remember your belief system doesn't have to be religious in nature (though for some of you, it will be), but that belief system provides you with the rules for functioning within the world. It may tell you how to treat others and how to expect them to treat you. It may tell you about the existence of right and wrong in the world, as well as the possibility of any gray areas. It may tell you whether things need to be proven or if they can be taken on faith. The importance is in living your life in a way that's consistent with your value system. It's super uncomfortable to be living in a way that doesn't hold up to the standards of your belief system and leaves you feeling either disconnected from your life or disconnected from your values.

Embrace the magic of your femininity. It is your God-given gift. Be empowered by your emotional capacity for kindness, compassion, and love. Don't look to equal yourself with a man, but rather establish yourself as a totally unique animal beyond comparison. Women must redefine the feminine, and we can only do so together. Smile at the next woman you see, compliment her shoes and let her know she is the most beautiful creature. By contributing love instead of fear to the community of women which you are a part of, you too will feel the beauty of being a strong woman. Practice courage and reflect your feminine light to the world!

Lindsey Shaw—actress

A true challenge for many is to be your true self. (Maybe even to figure out who she really is). Accept who you are—she's good enough just the way she is. All too often we try to change ourselves into what we believe we should be—either to match our own expectations or the expectations of others. This can happen in our comparison to men (or boys) too. There was a period of time where it was commonly believed that a woman had to become more masculine in order to succeed in the business world. She had to be hard and tough and often even went so far as to dress in menswear.

Google a movie from the '80s called *Working Girl*. The "successful" women in the film are initially cold and calculating and wear power suits with huge linebacker shoulder pads. You have to love '80s fashion...The less successful women (secretaries and assistants) wear '80s versions of feminine style—lots of makeup and miniskirts. Interestingly (spoiler alert), the main character learns that only in being herself personally, professionally, and stylishly, and not mimicking her mean boss, can she truly achieve real success. There's a key underlying message here—be yourself. Don't change to please other people, or you may not recognize yourself in the mirror.

Many see femininity as a spirituality all its own. There are even tons of religions that worship the female form. I think there can be a misperception of what femininity means. Often people will think of flowers and lace and pastel colors. That's only one facet of what femininity might mean. You, as a woman, get to define it in whatever terms you wish. You can, also, protect that right to define it for other women. You don't have to wear ribbons and lace to be feminine (though it's totally OK if you choose to do so). You can be just as feminine in a pair of jeans and a flannel shirt. Support that right in each other. You're part of a group that makes up 51 percent of the population.

There's power in your numbers, if only you will stick together. There's weakness if you, instead, tear each other down. You don't have to be ruthless to get ahead. Sure, plenty of ruthless people may have been able to claw themselves to some measure of success, but remember you need to be able to look yourself in the eye once you get there. Make decisions that support you becoming and maintaining the woman you want to be.

When I was in graduate school, there were two camps of students. Those who were out for themselves and would stab you in the back as soon as an opportunity arose and those who looked to work together for the benefit of all. People in both groups typically completed the program and achieved some form of success, but there were vast differences in how we perceived the process. You may have guessed that I was in the work together group—guilty! My classmates and I divided the work load and created study groups where we tutored each other and offered study help. We created deeper relationships with one another and frequently got together to hang out on weekends. We supported each other outside the classroom as well. Many of us still get together for mini reunions.

The lesson is this—both groups were able to complete the program, but in working together (almost becoming a team), we were able to make it easier, more pleasant, and, often times, more fun than it may otherwise have been. There are times in your life when you may have to compete, but, if possible, cooperation can be more beneficial. There's a saying that "many hands make light work," which basically means if we all work together, the work isn't as hard.

Follow Jesus as your Savior. His Ten Commandments will keep you safe. He will teach you about forgiveness and love (unconditional). Aloha.

Bethany Hamilton—professional surfer, author

I told you at the beginning of this chapter that this was about your value system and not any one specific religion. Bethany is known for her strong Christian beliefs almost as much as she's known for her surfing or her charitable works.

You can apply her words no matter what your religious beliefs might be. The Ten Commandments from the Bible can guide you about how to live your life in a positive way whether or not you're a Christian. The Commandments advise against stealing from, lying to, cheating on, murdering, or envying others. The Commandments stress the importance of respecting and treating your parents well. (As a mom, I support this!) These are decent life lessons—be truthful, be faithful, and try not to hurt others if you can help it. Many American laws are founded on similar principles.

Unconditional love is a hard one. If you're fortunate, you've been raised in a household that offers you unconditional love. Ideally, no matter how angry/frustrated/disappointed your parents may be with you sometimes, their love is always present. If you haven't been fortunate to know this love at home, I'm sorry. That sucks. I hope you can find it somewhere in your life—whether in friendship, a love relationship, with your future children, or in your relationship with whatever higher power you believe in. Everyone wants to know there's someone in this world who loves them no matter what they say or do. This doesn't mean you will necessarily support all of their choices, but you will love them anyway.

This is a frequent topic of discussion in our household. My daughter, sweetheart though she is, still gets into trouble once in a while (sometimes too often). This means we must be stern with her and offer some form of discipline that leaves her a little sad and often feeling like crud. I do my best to remind her that despite both of our roles in these interactions, I still love her. No matter what. I actually lead her through a conversation. It involves making sure she knows what she did wrong and why it was wrong. I give whatever punishment is appropriate to her misbehavior and then ask her if I still love her. She typically grumbles, "Yes." I then remind her that I will always love her no matter what...and I will. When I was a kid, my own mother used to say, "I don't necessarily like you right now, but I will always love you."

So much ... Most of all ... Hang in there...

Cat Deeley—television presenter, actress, singer, model

The title of this chapter says it all. I don't care what you believe in, but you need to believe in something. It doesn't matter if it's religion, femininity, sports, nature, music, art, something else, or all of the above. Just find something to believe in to help you through the tough spots. Whatever your belief system, it can help you understand the world you live in and why things happen the way they do. It can provide the moral compass by which you make your decisions. Find something to hold onto when things get hairy. Most of all, just hang on. Give things a chance to get better—they usually will.

Developing your moral compass:

1. **Be aware of the decisions you make each day**—big or small—and whether they're bringing you closer to or farther from the person you want to be. Look at the choices you've made in the past and consider whether or not you were following your morals at the time. Don't waste time feeling guilty if you failed to live up

to your morals. Vow to make changes in the future. You'll probably feel your self-confidence and personal strength growing as you face and overcome challenges in sticking to your values, whatever they may be.

2. **Consider the changes you may need to make in your future behaviors to more closely align your life with your moral compass**. Check to make sure your values are congruent with your behavior. As you grow, you may expand and deepen your value system. It's important to self-monitor to make sure your values are congruent with your behavior and thinking pattern. If not, it will create conflict, confusion, and maybe even anxiety and depression.

3. **Moral behaviors strengthen us as a community**. Know that what you do reflects on you and the people around you. Be responsible for your own actions, own up to your mistakes, and learn from them to be a better person.

4. **Beware of people who'll try to convince you to give up on your morals, saying that nobody's perfect, and taunting you for being such a goody-two-shoes**. The fact that nobody's perfect doesn't mean violating what you believe is right. It's good to learn from our mistakes, but we don't always need to make mistakes in order to learn. You have to have an individual sense of what it means to you to be moral. This can't be emulated. You can learn from others if it makes sense, but you have to build a moral compass for yourself. Don't step over other people's values. There's no moral

compass in place if you're stepping on other people's boundaries. If you have a compass, it may need some repairing before moving forward.

5. **You have to make sure you don't self-betray**. Never sell your integrity for anything. Know your ground, make it solid, and stay true to yourself. Have a clear boundary for protecting your integrity, and this will help activate your moral compass. People lose touch with their morality because they lose touch with their sense of integrity. You build a strong integrity by being consistent with your actions, measures, principles, expectations, and outcomes.

6. **Commit and you will get there**. Know there is no quick fix. You can't wake up and expect to have a clear sense of morality that you can automatically follow. There are stages to everything in life, and there are no escapes from these, in other words no short cuts. If you want to build a fully functioning compass, you have to walk the steps and work the work.

7. **Try not to take things too seriously.** Have a little laugh at your flaws (we all have them), and then try to fix them if you can. Don't take things as black and white; don't get fixated; open your mind to the variety and the beauty of life. Get yourself excited. If you lose something of value to you, give yourself time to grieve, process, and release the feeling, and bring the memory of love and joy to replace the pain. Make every moment count. This will help keep the compass clean.

8. **At the end, be flexible with the process**. Be sensitive to your needs and those of others. Plan your life so that you're full of life. Don't have unrealistic expectations. Focus on the process, not the outcome, and get excited. It will all come into focus over time.

Chapter 9
THE FUTURE

What the heck do I do now?

~~~~~~~~~~~~~~~~~~~~~~~

A ll things being equal, you have a long life ahead of you full of choices and decisions that need to be made. You don't need to be in any big hurry. All too often we can focus so much on what is coming next that we forget to enjoy what we have right now. I think the rush is something that happens to all of us. In elementary school, we can't wait until we can get into middle school. When we get to middle school, we're already planning for high school. You get to high school and you're looking forward to college and all the freedoms you'll finally have. In college, you can't wait until you're done and can make some "real money." This keeps going on and on and on…

Don't get me wrong, planning for your future is incredibly important—it's a really smart thing to do, but don't let your planning get in the way of enjoying what is going on for you right here and now. You've heard the phrase, "Stop and smell the roses," right? Do it! Take a moment and look around. Find all the wonderful things in your life right now. Celebrate them. You don't want to be sixty years old, planning for retirement, and realize you never enjoyed "the moment." Seems contradictory, huh? How can you plan for your future—set goals and all that we talked about in chapter 3—while seizing the moment? Like many things in life—it's all about balance. Plan and set goals but recognize and enjoy the here and now too.

> "It gets better" applies to everyone. Your options are about to open up, as long as you avoid choices now that will limit them.
>
> **Jane Espenson**—television writer and producer

The *It Gets Better Project* is a campaign aimed at LBGT teens who are struggling with society's reactions to their sexual orientation. The project's goal is to support these teens and reduce the heightened suicidality that exists in this population. Whether you're LGBT or not, the message remains the same. Your future is open to you and you have options available to make it better—not just for yourself, but for others as well. There's nothing worth killing yourself over. There's always a way out. Keep looking, asking, and begging until you find it.

You're the only one who can limit your future and, unfortunately, those limitations start being put into place now. What kinds of things can you do to limit your future? There are so many things—you can get arrested (for anything), do drugs that can lead to addiction or overdose, not take school seriously enough, have an unplanned or unwanted pregnancy, I could go on and on. It can be hard to think of your future plans when you're often living in the moment. Try as best as you can to remember that your choices in life either increase your future choices/options or narrow them. It kind of reminds me of those Choose Your Own Adventure books from when I was a kid. You would read along for a few pages and then a choice would be presented. If you choose option A, turn to page sixteen. If you choose option B, turn to page twenty-five. You'd keep reading from the page you selected until either another choice was presented or the story ended. Each choice you make now leads you to more of your life story and changes the future choices you'll have. Unfortunately, unlike the books, in real life we can't go back and make different choices to see how the story would have turned out. Make choices that leave you with paths open to your desired life path.

> Take your time. Don't rush into anything because you have the rest of your life ahead of you.
>
> **Stephany Alexander**—relationship, infidelity, and dating expert

We're always in such a rush to get to what is next! You (barring any major illness or unfortunate accident) have a long life ahead of you. You don't need to try to cram a lifetime worth of living into your first twenty-five years. Spread it out a little bit. You don't need to be in such a hurry to get to what's next. All too often I see people who have been in such a hurry that they didn't carefully consider their choices. There's no rush to get married, choose a career, or buy a house. You might choose foolishly if you don't give yourself enough time to consider your choices and figure out what you really want. There's a good reason most of us don't marry the person we dated when we were nineteen years old. Our "picker" may not yet be appropriately developed. At nineteen, I was still interested in guys that I could "fix"—damaged in some way and, often, not treating me very well. Thank God I didn't get my heart set on one of them—I don't imagine I would be in a happy, healthy relationship today.

Rushing too quickly into things can actually set you back. I've had a number of clients who were in such a hurry to be a grown-up that they tried to fast forward through all of their life experiences. They assumed that making adult decisions automatically made them adults. Not so fast. You can make grown-up decisions (sex, alcohol, babies) at any age and other decisions once you turn eighteen (marriage, credit cards, military). Just because you can and might make these choices, doesn't make you grown. I know too many people who tried to find a short cut to adulthood and ended up broke, divorced, and/or in rehab. You have your whole life for the adult stuff. In fact, the majority of your years will be spent in adulthood. Take your time—it's not a race.

Enjoy each moment; try not to be in a rush to grow up. Each moment is precious and is an opportunity for growth.

Desi Lydic—actress

My daughter and I were out for dinner one night, and as we were walking along she turned to me and said she couldn't wait until she was a mom someday. She told me it would be fun to be the one who could make all the decisions. She even gave me the example that her daughter would ask her if she could have chocolate and she would let her "sometimes" because too often would make her sick. I applauded her for her fair response—because everyone should be able to have chocolate sometimes—but also told her to slow down. I even gave her examples of things she would have to give up when she's a mom (i.e., having me and her dad do all of her cooking and laundry). There's tons of time to be a mom in the future; she should enjoy being the kid while she can. Now she's only eight years old, but the idea is true for you too.

Enjoy being a teenager/young adult while you can. For some reason, we all think there's some other age when things were magically perfect. My daughter thinks it will be when she's a mom. (I can only hope it lives up to her expectations.) I have friends who look back on their teen years and remember them as somehow perfect. They have this idealized image of someone else doing their laundry, paying the bills, cooking dinner, and making all of the decisions. To them, this sounds like a stress-free existence. You probably just snorted in disgust, didn't you? You know how hard it can be not to have control over your own life and to have other people make your choices for you. Keep your perspective. There's no perfect time in your life—enjoy where you are now and make the best of it while you're there.

> Being a teenager is awesome. Being an adult sucks (ha ha).
>
> **Ellie Goulding**—singer-songwriter

It's all about perspective. Remember? My daughter, Charlie, wants to be a grown-up because of the freedom and being able to be the one who makes decisions. My friends want to be teenagers again so they won't have as many responsibilities. Recently, Charlie and I went out to dinner and the greeter asked Charlie what grade she was in. Charlie said she was in third. Then the greeter (who was a junior in high school) said she wished she was back in third grade. We all want to be some other age/stage than the one we're in. Enjoy where you are. Each age has its own good and bad parts. As for the future, we'll all get there—eventually.

> Be very careful when deciding your firsts, for they set the bar of your future baggage. #FirstLove, #FirstJob, #FirstKiss, etc.
>
> **Alice Greczyn**—actress and model

You're at a point in your life where there are still a number of firsts ahead of you, though some may have already passed. I recommend that you take care in choosing your firsts—once they're done, they're done, and you can't undo them. This applies to your first love and first sexual partner (not always the same person), your first act of real rebellion, and your first home away from home, to name a few. If you aren't careful, you may find you've set yourself up to be disappointed. This isn't the end of the world.

This is a learning opportunity. If you want to be self-destructive, you can allow your firsts to become baggage—either because they were so good or so bad, or you can choose to learn from them and use them to make positive future decisions. You might be confused—how can good firsts become baggage? Well, if your first love was a positive, happy relationship, you might build them up so much that no other love can ever compare and may feel like less because of it. This can make it difficult to ever allow yourself to be satisfied with anyone else.

I've observed this happening in my practice with a number of firsts (or sometimes even seconds or thirds). I've had clients who have lost their dream job (for a number of reasons) and have built that job up to have been so perfect for them that no other job can ever make them happy. I've worked with clients who are unable to let go of "the one," the ex-boyfriend or ex-girlfriend, who completed them in a way that no one else ever can. What can happen to these people if we don't intervene? They give up. Why look for a new job if the perfect one has already been and gone? Why go out on dates if their soul mate has already been and gone? My dearies get out of your own way. Dump that baggage. Figure out what you liked about the job or person and try to find it elsewhere. The fact that you found it once is proof that it exists and means it's possible to find again.

This also happens in the reverse. Say you have a horrible relationship—it's abusive, unfaithful, and/or generally damaging, or you have a horrible job experience—your boss is cruel, dishonest, and/or inappropriate. This might cause you to sour on the ideas of new relationships or jobs (or whatever bad experience you may have had). You may decide to avoid them going forward. You might be surprised how many people following a bad relationship will tell me they intend to remain single forever—and they mean it! A bad relationship is not an indicator that relationships are bad, just that one you were in with that person.

A bad job experience doesn't mean working will necessarily be a bad experience in the same way that having a bad time with a specific food means you should never eat again. Let me give you an example. My roommate in college got a horrible case of the stomach flu. She was sick all over the place and the last food she'd eaten prior to getting sick was pizza. For years after, she couldn't stand the idea of pizza. The sight, smell, and taste made her instantly nauseous. She didn't quit eating all together; she just avoided the specific food that upset her. Your ex-boyfriend or girlfriend is like that pizza. Maybe you need to avoid him or her, but you can still enjoy all the other options available out there. There are a lot of choices available on the menu.

The sky is the limit to what you can achieve. Always work hard, stay humble, and be grateful.

JoAnna Garcia—actress

No one can or should set limits on what you can become. Why? Because there's no way to know how far you can go until you've tried to get there. If you're willing to work hard and take reasonable risks, you'll accomplish much. Remember that long life span you have in front of you? You'll have all of that time to continue to learn and grow. Don't give up just because others are not sure you can make it. If you still want it, keep working. Push through those barriers.

Do you want to know the hardest part about becoming a success? It isn't the hard work it takes to get there. It isn't the sacrifices you might need to make. The biggest challenge is not allowing your success to go to your head and make you someone you're not. Someone you may not want to be. You don't want to be an arrogant ass. How can you avoid this? Be humble and be grateful. Appreciate all that has been done to help you on your way. Recognize the role good luck can play in your success. Remember all those who gave you a boost when you needed some support. What does humble mean? It means not being proud or arrogant in the face of your success. Remember and appreciate all of the help you received along the way.

Charlie recently tried out for the school talent show—a very big deal for the elementary set. Anyway, a classmate came out after completing her audition and Charlie and a friend ran up to ask her how it had gone. This little girl snapped her fingers in their faces and said, "You know I killed it!" Part of me wanted to applaud her self-confidence, a quality that can carry her far in a world that may try to knock her down. But another part of me cringed. This just seemed so booger-snotty. I'm afraid it makes life (and other kids) want to smack her down.

It did become a great "teachable moment" for me and for my daughter. We talked about the importance of being confident but humble. We talked about various alternative responses a person might give when asked how her audition had gone and settled on something that felt more comfortable for her. ("I did my best and I think it went pretty well"). Something different might work best for you, just consider your audience. You don't need to trash yourself—that always seems a little sad to me, but you also don't have to toot your own horn. If you're awesome, others will recognize your greatness; you don't need to rub their noses in it.

> Do not believe anyone who tries to tell you what you can't do or be or achieve. Especially don't believe the people who love you and tell you those things. Their motives are good but their worldview is limited. Thank them, love them, and keep yourself on the course of achieving your dreams. Because your dreams are possible. Anything is possible. Know that.
>
> **Krista Vernoff**—writer and producer

The people we love are sometimes not our biggest cheerleaders. This isn't necessarily because they don't love us. Sometimes they might love us too much. This seems strange, right? If they love us, they should only want the best for us and for us to achieve all of our dreams. The problem is they sometimes want to protect us. They can be afraid for us to reach for the stars because we may fall on our faces, and they don't want us to be disappointed or experience the pain. Remember how I said you sometimes need to get out of your own way? Well, sometimes you might need to push your loved ones out of your way too. Please remember to do it respectfully. Appreciate that their love is what is making them try to protect you from yourself and the sadness the world has to offer. You want these people to be there for you whether you succeed or fail. There's no need to alienate them as you strive to achieve your dreams.

Your loved ones may also have limited experiences that cause them to believe your dreams are not possible. When I was little, we lived in low-income housing. Most of the families in my neighborhood often had working class jobs in careers that required very little formal education. I grew up in suburban Detroit; so many people worked in the auto industry and were happy to have the good paying jobs that the factories provided with benefits that helped take care of their families. I'm not knocking these people in any way. They paid their bills, loved their families and raised good kids.

What I did notice, though, is some families did not value education beyond high school. They believed their children would be best served by graduating high school and getting in with a union job as soon as they could after graduation. They discouraged their children from going to college and viewed it as a waste of time and money. Some thought their kids were being "uppity" for wanting to go to college. I'm going to tell you the same thing I would've told them—your dreams are your own. It doesn't matter if you want to work in the factory, in the hospital or on the stage. You can achieve them if you're willing to work hard and put in the necessary effort. If your loved ones are not on board, keep the lines of communication open and, hopefully, they'll cheer louder than anyone else when you get there.

Realize that your life will NOT always be the way it is right now!

Liz Brown—writer and comedian

Your life can change in so many ways—some within your control and some far outside it. The things you can't control include such things as other people's thoughts, feelings, and behaviors, to name a few. Those situations outside your control are, well, outside your control, so let's not focus on those. You'll just have to learn how to survive those with as little lasting damage as possible. Fortunately, there are so many things that are within your control. Your life will not always be the way it is today. You want to know why? Because you can change it! If you don't like your current circumstances, start making some changes and keep tweaking things until you're satisfied with how things stand. Is it ever going to be perfect? Unlikely, but "good enough" can feel pretty darn great.

Figure out what you want and then starting making a plan to get there. Remember the goal planning from chapter 2? Use it! If you don't like your job, then start looking for one where you can do what you actually want and get whatever education, training, or connections you might need to get it. Not thrilled with your social circumstances (otherwise known as not loving your friends or boyfriend/girlfriend), then start expanding your social network. Meet new people. Figure out how to connect with people you actually have something in common with or might reasonably like. In a nutshell, if you don't like it, find a way to change it. Your future can be different from your present. The biggest factor in what that future might be is you. Get off your butt and start making some moves.

The best people have miserable adolescences. :) It gets better. Do charity work for perspective. Talk to yourself like you are your BFF.

Kate Dillion—model, activist, and humanitarian

How many times have we heard from famous people that their adolescence was one of torture? They were social outcasts, not asked to the prom, and were bullied by their peers. It can be hard to relate to them when they're now successful, wealthy, and beautiful, but it may have been true when they were teens. It's important to remember that if you're not enjoying your teen years as much as you had hoped, you're not alone in this. Studies show roughly 20percent of teenagers are suffering from emotional "issues" including anxiety and depression. There are tons of reasons for this, including, but not limited to, social dynamics, family issues, plain old hormones, and all that puberty crap.

The good news is much of this gets better with time. Your hormones will balance out (and so will those of your friends and boyfriends/girlfriends). You'll be able to move away (either physically or emotionally) from friends and family if they're challenging for you. (College can be an ideal safety hatch.) This stuff gets better as people around you (sometimes slowly) begin to mature and become more "human." You will too.

There have been people in my life with whom I've chosen to stop spending time—friends, family, and coworkers. Each circumstance has its own explanation, but in each situation I decided that continuing the relationship would do me more harm than good. Sometimes continuing the relationships might have placed my daughter at risk for emotional harm. It doesn't mean there had to be a big, ugly fight that signaled the end. Rather, I usually let them fade away. There doesn't have to be anger and hurt feelings, but instead you need to focus on a healthier life and a healthier future.

The challenge is to find a way to maintain your perspective while you're waiting for things to "get better." You can always sit back and wait for it to happen—which might be a long, rather boring wait—or you can distract yourself by helping others out. Volunteering to help others is great for you for two reasons. First, you'll be so busy while you're volunteering that you can't focus on yourself for just a little while. You'll be distracted from your own crap, kind of like giving yourself a vacation from your own problems.

Secondly (and maybe most importantly), helping others can force you to realize that you may not have it that bad. You may find a new perspective on your own life. There are others who may be worse off than you—you can almost always think of at least one. This might help you to appreciate those things in your life that aren't so terrible.

I mentioned earlier that when I was in elementary and junior high school, my mom was married to a bad guy. He wasn't bad all of the time, sometimes he was nice, but when he was mad—watch out. He was also an alcoholic, so you can imagine the disaster of mixing a bad temper with a substance abuse problem. There were many times during those years when I thought things couldn't get any worse and wondered what I had done to get so screwed. Then when I was in seventh grade (I think), a girl from my class died from cancer. It helped me put things in proper perspective. Now it didn't make me happily dance around excited to have an angry, drunk stepfather, but I did realize I was (at least) still alive.

I started counting down days, months, and years until I could go away to college and leave him in the dust. Fortunately for me, we got out when I was in ninth grade after I called the police in the middle of the night while he was on a drunken tear through the house. I didn't have to survive those additional three years, five months, and fourteen days under the same roof with him. I received an early reprieve. If things are bad, remember they could always be worse and for some people, they already are. The future can be better for you. If your safety is ever a concern, ask for help and keep asking until it finally arrives. I can tell you that when it was time for me to start dating, I made sure substance abuse and anger management issues were an automatic deal breaker.

What's awful now will one day be hilarious.

Laura Brown—features/special projects and executive director of *Harper's Bazaar* magazine

Some of my favorite life anecdotes started out as terrible experiences. Time can make them funny for you and others. Give yourself a chance to find the distance to allow them to become comical. Some of my most painful breakup stories are now hilarious. I can laugh at moments of teenage rebellion where I was so self-righteous in my anger. (Remember my geometry teacher?) Understand that time doesn't take all of the pain away, but it allows you the perspective to view it from all sides— including the laughable. If something happens that hurts your feelings, chalk it up to life experience. It will be a funny footnote in your autobiography someday. You and your friends will enjoy swapping stories over a glass of wine someday—cracking each other up at your examples of your misspent youth.

Don't worry, you'll be older soon!

Milla Jovovich—model, actress, musician, and fashion designer

How to live in the moment:

1. **Ignore your audience and dance like no one's watching**. While you may or may not like dancing, whether or not anyone is watching, the idea sums up the idea of living in the moment. Little kids don't worry about the future; they play and enjoy every moment for what it is. They haven't yet learned to think ahead, or agonize over the past, so take the opportunity to learn from them.

2. **Think positively**. If you care—if you even give a thought to—who's looking, you're performing. Your goal is to impress (or at least not disappoint) your audience. To live in the moment, to "dance like nobody's watching," you have to forget about performing for others and simply accept the moment for what it is. Dance for your enjoyment. Focus on how it feels to move your body—not how it looks. It can bring you in the moment and increase your confidence.

3. **Pay attention to the world around you.** No matter what you're doing, notice the moments that surround you. Maybe on your way to work or school, you go down a tree-lined street or you get a view of the sun rising over the mountains. Smell the freshly mown grass (one of my personal favorites). Feel the warmth of the sun on your face. When I was a kid, we would occasionally drive past this farm where they raised a variety of animals. Every time we drove by, my mom would roll down the windows and take a big whiff of the air and a smile would light up her face. The heavenly aroma? Cow manure. Seriously. Stinky. Yuck. To my mom, though, it was the smell of my great grandparents' farm and her childhood. Stop and smell the manure (or the roses, whichever you prefer).

4. **Pay attention to whatever you're doing.** Even if you're just walking, or wiping the counter, or shuffling cards—how does it feel? There's probably some kind of internal dialogue running through your mind, and it probably has to do with something other than

what you're doing. Let those thoughts go and focus on what *is* (not what *was* or what *could be*). Examine your breath; by noticing your breathing pattern, your mind naturally quiets and pays more attention to the present moment. Remember productiveness isn't always beneficial. It's great to get stuff done, but sometimes it's even better to sit back and lose yourself in something that has no measurable result, something that's simply fun. **You don't need to spend every moment of your life getting things done**. (I still need to work on this one.)

5. **Strive to find balance.** Anything in excess is dangerous. Practice the art of work-life separation and strive to do everything in moderation. When you introduce balance into your life, you become more aware of what you're doing, giving you a chance to accept moments for what they are. Don't let anything consume your life. There is such a thing as too much of a good thing.

6. **Start your day off with a smile**. You can set the mood for the next twenty-four hours by simply waking up and smiling. Don't wake up with a groan and throw your alarm clock against the wall. There's scientific proof that your facial expressions can actually influence how you feel. The mere act of smiling (even if you aren't necessarily feeling it) can release chemicals in your brain that can actually make you feel happier. Roll over, give yourself a good stretch, and focus on the good things that can happen to you today. Find ways to forgive others. Many of us carry grudges with us

that haunt us, and those grudges also prevent us from finding happiness. It's hard to smile if you're focused on the wrongs others may have done to you.

7. **Seek out opportunities to commit random acts of kindness.** Whether it's donating a dollar to the guy collecting money for the homeless outside the grocery store, picking up litter, or helping victims of natural disasters, keep alert in each moment of your day for some way that you can make the world a better place. Even the smallest thing, like complimenting someone, can bring joy. It's the most spontaneous and unexpected act of kindness that produces the greatest impact, and you can't be sensitive to those kinds of opportunities unless you're living in the moment. A friend recently shared how she had let a car merge in front of her at a Starbucks drive-thru recently. She thought nothing of the act; she simply let the driver into her lane despite the fact that it might set her back a few minutes. When she approached the drive-thru window, she learned the other driver had paid for her coffee as a thank you. These two relatively simple acts left both feeling positive and pleased with their fellow man. It was then posted on my friend's Facebook page and, hopefully, inspired others to be more considerate of one another. Your random act of kindness can lead to a series of similar actions.

8. **Reduce activities that dull your awareness of "the moment."** What are you doing that tempts your mind to run away from the present? For most people,

watching television leaves you near comatose and time slips right by. Daydreaming and getting lost in a good movie or book isn't bad, but it's not living in the moment because it places your concentration on something that isn't right here, right now; it's a form of escapism. How many times have you gone online and when you next looked up, realized hours had gone by? Don't tune out; tune *in*. Do things that are active, encourage you to look around, and engage the world in that moment. Going for a run, interacting with a friend, spending some time outdoors, and creating art (music, painting, writing, etc.) are all activities that lend themselves to mindfulness. Participate in active conversation and engage in the subject matter with another human. This should be an actual conversation with an actual person—no texting, instant messages, or email. Your biggest time suck—technology. Take a break from the Internet, TV, and radio so you can be aware of what's going on right now in the present moment of your life.

9. **Appreciate what is**. When you find yourself wishing for something you don't have, or wishing your life could be different, start your journey for your wish by being thankful for what is already in your life. This will bring you back to the present moment. Make a list of what you're thankful for right now, even if all you can think of is that you are alive and can breathe. You don't want to miss the good things right in front of you because you're always looking beyond what's in the

present moment to what once was or what might be. If you're thankful for what is, you'll be happy to be in the moment—instead of dreaming about being happy someplace else.

CONCLUSION

I sit here wondering what I want to say to you as the final message of this book. I feel like it should somehow be something profound to effectively tie it all together. I can't help but think of the wonderful women who have contributed to this book's creation and offered such impressive advice to you (with absolutely no compensation beside the possibility of being able to help you), and I struggle with how to wrap it all up in a nice neat little bow. My temptation is to pick out my favorite quotes, but I don't want to highlight any one person's words because doing so would somehow lessen everyone else's. Instead, I'm going to give you a list of take away messages that are written in no particular order:

1. Believe in yourself. You are awesome.
2. Be patient. Most people will be less jerk-like as they age. Most, not all.
3. You know best what you need. Trust yourself.
4. Turn something you love into a career. It will make going to work suck less.
5. Do things that scare you. It can be exciting.
6. No naked pictures **EVER**! They'll bite you in the butt.
7. Enjoy each moment.
8. Everything gets easier. Give it a chance.
9. Check yourself before you criticize anyone else. You may be just as guilty as they are.
10. No one is perfect. No one. Not even celebrities.
11. You can always change your mind. Anytime. Anywhere.
12. Make embarrassing moments funny. They can't make fun of you if you're already laughing.
13. No naked pictures **EVER**! Seriously, I mean it.
14. Make your choices wisely. You have to live with the consequences.
15. Be yourself. You're worth being.
16. Learn to deal with people who are pains in the ass. You'll meet others like them later.
17. You'll find your groove. Just keep dancing.
18. Use caution posting things on the Internet. They can definitely come back to haunt you.
19. Connect with your higher power.
20. Hard work is required and it pays off.
21. Value yourself. You're worth it.

22. Talk about money. Use your negotiating power.
23. Stand up for other girls. We need to have each other's backs.
24. No naked pictures **EVER!** You never know where they might turn up.
25. Understand the value of money. Working helps here.
26. Embrace life. You only get one.
27. Your dreams are possible. You just need to make them happen.
28. Others' opinions do not matter. You decide what is right and wrong for you.
29. Keep your eye on the prize. It can help keep you moving forward.
30. Ask for what you want. You just might get it.
31. No naked pictures **EVER!** They rarely stay private.
32. Save something out of every dollar you earn. You'll be happy when an unexpected expense comes up.
33. Follow your moral compass. It will keep you on track.
34. Treat yourself like a best friend. Unconditional love at its best.
35. Love yourself. You need to do this to be able to love others.
36. You can achieve anything with hard work. Sometimes it's REALLY hard work.
37. Have fun. You need to balance all that hard work.
38. You can't buy happiness—just more debt.
39. No naked pictures **EVER!** You give your power away.
40. Embrace your femininity. You are woman, hear you roar.

41. You will someday laugh about it (and it won't be a fake laugh either).
42. Don't be a victim to the trends. Be yourself no matter what you wrap yourself in.
43. Be unafraid. There is strength in taking chances.
44. Focus on the things you can control. Everything else is someone else's problem.
45. Hang in there. Give it a chance to turn around.
46. Mean girls are insecure. They're trying to make themselves feel better by trashing you.
47. No naked pictures **EVER**! I can't stress this enough.
48. You're important. You matter.
49. Do what makes you happy and proud. It can make the hard work feel less hard.
50. Be thankful. Appreciating what you have makes missing what you don't less terrible.
51. It gets better. Give it some time.
52. Surround yourself with supporters. It can't hurt to have your own personal cheering section.
53. Trust your gut. It's trying to tell you something important.
54. Choose a career you believe in and enjoy. If you have to go there every day, you might as well not be miserable.
55. No naked pictures **EVER**! Are you getting the picture yet?
56. Mistakes and challenges will shape you. Sometimes for the better.

57. Take your time. You have a long life ahead of you—there doesn't need to be any rush.
58. Your sexual energy is powerful. Choose how to use it best.
59. Follow your heart. It's strong.
60. You can be and do anything. Just keep trying and don't give up.
61. Let go of your fears. They may be holding you back.
62. Perspective is everything. Sometimes a little distance can make it all a little clearer.
63. Finally—no naked pictures **EVER**!

Ultimately the most important thing to remember is that you're important, you matter, and you have the right to be respected. You'll teach others how to treat you. Teach them well. You deserve it and…No naked pictures **EVER**!

ABOUT THE AUTHOR

 Kelly Tonelli is a clinical psychologist working in private practice with patients who are experiencing life transitions, many of whom are teenage girls. She happily relocated from Michigan to Southern California to attend Pepperdine University and fell in love with the sunshine (snow is cold). She's been fortunate to have spent time working and learning at Children's Hospital of Los Angeles (CHLA) before going into private practice. She divides her time between her practice, writing, spending time with her husband, and driving her daughter to dance class.

INDEX

Alexander, Stephany, 128

Bearman, Erika, 12
Bravo, Maria, 78
Brown, Laura, 140
Brown, Liz, 137
Burch, Tory, 4

Carpenter, Jennifer, 58
Chung, Alexa, 107
Curry, Ann, 46

Deeley, Cat, 122
Dillon, Kate, 138
Dushku, Eliza, 33

Eisner, Stacey Bendet, 79
Elliot, Missy, 9
Espenson, Jane, 127

Flanders, Cait, 90

Garcia, JoAnna, 133
Goulding, Ellie, 131
Graham, Kat, 6
Grandin, Temple, 40
Greczyn, Alice, 131

Hamilton, Bethany, 120
Hasselbeck, Elisabeth, 80

Jenkins, Jeannette, 114

Jenkins, Kaitlyn, 13

Jovovich, Milla, 141

Kerr, Hillary, 31

Leive, Cindi, 21

London, Stacy, 106

Lydic, Desi, 130

Malone, Jena, 60

McCarthy, Jenny, 11

McCord, AnnaLynne, 29

McKellar, Danica, 67

Neilan, Lisa Cochran, 60

Nguyen, Janet, 75

Olen, Helaine, 91

Pace, Natalie, 92

Pratt, Allana, 23, 115

Priesand, Rabbi Sally J., 99

Quick, Becky, 87

Ronson, Samantha, 14

Sanford, Kiki, 47

Scerbo, Cassie, 102

Shaw, Lindsey, 118

Smirnoff, Karina, 116

Sweeney, Anne-Marie, 65

Teegarden, Aimee, 74

Travis, Brooke K., 63

Van, Jessika, 105

Vernoff, Krista, 135

Walters, Lisa Anne, 27

Walters, Mimi, 43

Weston, Liz Pulliam, 88

White, Vanna, 59

Wilkerson, Carrie, 20